Ploughshare
to
Crook

A farmer's boy from Somerset, Bill Flagg went to
South America in 1951 and became bishop of a new
diocese of Paraguay and northern Argentina in 1969.
Subsequently, as bishop in Peru and a presiding
bishop in South America, he served on the Anglican
Consultative Council and its sub committees which
gave him first-hand knowledge of the Church in
Australia, Africa, Asia and North America.

He has also served in the diocese of Liverpool
and as general secretary of the South American
Missionary Society before moving to the diocese of
Southwell (Nottinghamshire), where he lives in active
retirement. He has six children and eleven grandchildren.

Bill has written numerous articles on missiology
and other subjects, but *From Ploughshare to Crook* is
his first book.

Dedication

I dedicate this book to my darling wife Marj, who died just as it was going to press. Self-effacing and unselfish to the end, she taught us much about holy living, and holy dying.

From Ploughshare to Crook

Bill Flagg's Story

BILL FLAGG

TRIANGLE

Published in Great Britain in 2000 by
Triangle
Society for Promoting Christian Knowledge
Holy Trinity Church
Marylebone Road
London NW1 4DU

British Library Cataloguing-in-Publication Data

A catalogue record for this book is available
from the British Library

ISBN 0-281-05213-1

Typeset by Pioneer Associates, Perthshire
Printed in Great Britain by
Caledonian International, Glasgow

CONTENTS

FOREWORD

One of my enthusiasms over many years has been 'second chance learning'.

Bishop Bill Flagg is an outstanding example of someone who missed out on formal education after 14 years of age, but who has had far-reaching influence in God's kingdom. This story of the adventurous life of this modest man will bring encouragement to many who are tempted to 'put themselves down' rather than acknowledge that God has given them their own special gifts.

A loving home, where 'Dad never expected me to say no to any task', was an important base for this resourceful life. So was the lively community of a village, where a garage mechanic taught him all about reconditioning machines and keeping them in good mechanical order. It's not every bishop on his confirmation tour who is competent at crawling under the jeep to mend the steering. When he came to Liverpool, within months the vicarage garden was producing all the vegetables the Flagg family could want.

This farmer's boy used all the gifts he'd learned in an English village – managing a farm, crossing wide areas of Chile on horseback, not to mention the hair-raising train and bus journeys across South America's great distances. Bill Flagg tells that story vividly, and, along with it, the spiritual adventure of lifelong learning of the life of faith. Along with Bill's adventurous spirit we receive glimpses of the courage, wisdom and spirituality of his wife, Marj, who shared the adventure and paid much of the cost.

This adventure story tells of pioneer missionary work being given lasting foundations. Bill has been a builder in practical and spiritual senses, always having an eye to the need for continuity in work that may have been started by rugged individualists. Whether he was in rural Indian communities, in the pueblos jovenes, housing millions around the edges of South American cities, or in the inner city in Liverpool, he insisted that the Gospel is for the un-bookish, who have often felt themselves excluded. There are important insights to be found in Bill's description of his learning, in Paraguay and in Peru, to be gentle in his use of authority; in unchurched, but sort-of-believing England, he insisted that the sacraments of baptism and holy communion should not be used as instruments of discipline: 'God has given them as instruments of mission for seekers in a needy world.'

Often there had been little expectation that local leadership could be established. The book shows Bill's commitment to the belief that God has given gifts that can be developed in every community. He played a major part in developing the SEAN (Seminary by Extension to All Nations) courses that have become world-wide and ecumenical tools of developing second chance learning for those who have lacked opportunities before.

Bill Flagg saw the importance of the quest for unity in the Church from early in his ministry. In South America, as in Liverpool, people were not likely to believe if they saw Protestants and Roman Catholics at each other's throats. Taking part as a new bishop in the meeting between ten Roman Catholic and ten Anglican bishops in 1970 opened up whole new possibilities of Christian recognition and partnership, which he has followed up consistently.

This is the account of a missionary statesman; when he was first made a bishop in South America, he immediately understood the challenge of relating the diocese to the World Church. When I visited Argentina and Peru in 1982 for the establishment of the Anglican Province of the Southern Cone, I saw for myself the vision that Bill and others had worked for, of the church that had been English-speaking becoming Spanish-speaking, coming true. That was always necessary, if the church was to be seen as open for the main population.

When he went from Liverpool to be general secretary of the South American Missionary Society (SAMS), the society knew that they were appointing someone who would insist that they listened to the national leaders of the young churches. No longer were missionaries from Europe to go as agents of the society; now SAMS was described as an agent of the Anglican Churches in South America.

I gladly commend this account, always told with a generous spirit, and with a twinkling eye. We bounce along at a rare pace, as if we are in the saddle with Bishop Bill, crossing the great distance of South America, but we learn significant lessons of discipleship and church-building as we go.

The Rt Revd Lord David Sheppard of Liverpool

PREFACE

It is many moons since Lord Donald Coggan, the then Archbishop of Canterbury, suggested that in my idle moments I should pen my story. Thankfully, idle moments have seldom come my way, but a publisher did, and I am grateful to Alison Barr, SPCK's commissioning editor, for keeping my nose to the grindstone with her helpful suggestions.

The reduction of my original 80,000 words to less than half means that I have failed to name many friends, particularly those within the SAMS (South American Missionary Society) family, such as the late Canon Robert Smith, who was like an older brother in the Lord to me. Nor could I relate important happenings like the Liverpool riots, or Dr Billy Graham's Mission England in 1984.

The task was made all the more enjoyable by my late wife Marj's consistent encouragement and the fact that Bishop David Evans, the general secretary of SAMS, feels that this book may be useful to the society. My hope and prayer is that it will encourage others to trust and serve the Lord Jesus Christ.

Who answers Christ's insistent call,
Must give himself, his life, his all,
Without one backward look.
Who puts his hand unto the plough
And looketh back with anxious brow,
His calling hath forsook.

Anon

1
SOMERSET

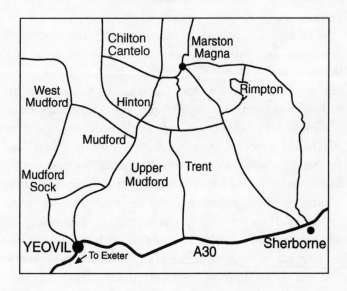

From milkboy to bishop

Mother was upset because our local paper had captioned my appointment 'From milkboy to bishop'. After all, what was wrong with being a milkboy? She had more reason to be upset by a letter from one of our missionaries. His intended thank you letter following a visit was probably very courteous, but she received one that should have gone into another envelope. It read, 'I visited the Flagg family and was surprised to find that Bishop Flagg had grown up in a council house!' So what was wrong with a council house? I remember Mother using the communal pump, which served ten homes prior to the installation of running water, but it was a very nice clean and comfortable home. Situated at the top of the village of Mudford in Somerset, it overlooked the manor farm, across the valley to the village of Trent where Charles II hid while escaping to France.

Our house, 2 Hill View, was one of the first six council houses to be built in our village between the wars. The living room had an old-fashioned kitchen range, later replaced by an open fire. Mum used a two-chimney paraffin cooker and oven in summertime. The kitchen took the first impact of muddy boots and wet clothes. It had a copper which was used on Mondays for washing day, Saturdays for heating water to be carried upstairs for the weekly baths, and around 'Stir up Sunday'[1] for making Christmas puddings. The cool larder under the stairs also served as an air raid shelter during the war years. Our diet was wholesome and healthy with vegetables from the garden, home-made butter and plenty of eggs, rabbits and poultry. The smell of 'Mansion' furniture polish, from Mother's hard work to keep everything clean, mingled with smells of cooking.

No one can choose their parents, but I certainly would not choose to be born into any other family, in any other place or time.

Village life

Mudford, like any other village, had its craftsmen and its characters. The Flagg clan produced the characters. Granny Flagg raised 11 children. One of the four boys was a Methodist local preacher, whose plaque in the little village chapel, after his death as a soldier in the First World War, inspired me greatly. His name was also in the brass plaque in church along with all the others that perished in conflict. Granny was an imaginative entrepreneur and my earliest memory of work was helping Dad load her pigs into the spring wagon[2] ready for market. Pig-keeping was one of several sidelines in her struggle to raise the family. Sadly, Grandad Flagg died when I was eight.

Granny Hawkins, like my mother, was a sweet lady, and the holidays I spent at her small, West Coker Hill farmhouse were great fun. I once got so carried away playing with my uncle that I jumped out of a low bedroom window on to his back. An incident well remembered because of Uncle Ern's shock, rebuke and the legend it created! I was named John William Hawkins after my grandfather, who died of cancer just before my birth. He had bought a small farm at West Coker Hill. A photo of him, standing upright beside his saddled horse, with a double watch chain on his waistcoat and wearing leather gloves, portrays a degree of affluence for his day. Mother wistfully told me that had Grandad Hawkins lived, Dad would have received more help in his early days of farming. Grandad had told mother that he preferred Dad's little finger to the whole of her previous boyfriend!

My father had a temper but he only hit me once. It seems that at the age of eight I had become increasingly difficult to get to bed. I hated being called in from play across the road where we gathered conkers and climbed our favourite tree. I was in the armchair, kicking out at Mother who wanted to take off my boots, when there was a click of the kitchen door latch and Father stormed in with some thick string, which he happened to be carrying.

It served the purpose of whipping my legs below the short trousers, as I wriggled and writhed in the chair. That was a lesson not forgotten, but what impressed my young mind more was that when it was over and the tears had dried, I was not put to bed, but walked across the fields with Dad to shut up the hens for the night. The lesson that day was of my father's love.

By some standards life was tough. Dad never expected me to say 'no' to any task, however difficult. He drove himself hard and expected the same commitment from others. It must have been a family trait. Grandparents on both sides of the family started as farm labourers, yet four of their sons became farmers in their own right. In Dad's time, clever children took an examination at 12. Those who passed could choose to leave school, and that's what he chose. Mr Stockley, our blacksmith, told me how Dad first worked as his assistant for two weeks. 'He was a good little lad but hardly stiff enough for the work.' He did much better at Trent farm where he became a responsible cowman at the age of 16.

From the age of ten I would enjoy taking our farm-horses, Prince and Punch, to the blacksmith's shop. It was my job to work the bellows and I watched closely as the shoes were hammered out on the anvil. I would then crawl around to blacken the horses' hoofs with waste oil, to make them look respectable as they were led back to the muddy farm.

Many years later, when he was blind and in his nineties, Mr Stockley knew how to humble a young bishop. 'Let me feel your hands, Billy boy.' My hands, which had been rough and tough in my teens, were now softened. 'That won't do, Billy Boy, your hands be too soft. You ain't done no work lately!' My dad took a different line. He always maintained that 'paper work' could be just as exhausting as physical labour and wanted me to learn, but he rightly insisted that farming demanded as much, if not more, skill and versatility than most professions.

One summer's evening in 1938 we watched a German flying ship on its so-called friendship visit. The photos it took then were probably used for bombing raids later and would have served Germany well had the invasion taken place. We were harvesting oats when Hitler invaded Poland on 1 September 1939. Dad optimistically expounded the Polish capacity to fight as he drove to the cornfield in his Ford car, with its tyres worn down to the canvas. What a mixed memory of a ten year old's experience this is! After the 'phoney war', when nothing seemed to happen, Hitler's troops ignored the impregnable French Maginot Line by marching through Belgium,[3] and in a short time our troops were providentially escaping back across the channel. Dogfights took place in the sky above us, as lone bombers would creep in for daylight raids.

Dad had wanted to join the army, but farming was a priority occupation and he was told to stay on the farm. In those days it was possible to build up in farming as Dad did, first by renting a bit of land alongside the railway track, plus some allotments, and then the grazing rights of a 4-acre field. By the time he married he had saved enough money to rent a county council small-holding and he was given the treasured tenancy of the council house as part of the package. Between the wars the county councils bought over 3,000 small-holdings that were let out to enterprising people in the hope that the tenancy would be a first step towards establishment in larger farms. Only 50 or so managed to expand beyond the council property. My father was one of them. He bought his first field, for £100 an acre, before I was 13. He was lucky that other adjoining fields gradually came on the market and he was pleased that he could actually hold the deeds because he paid cash down.

Muscles from milking gave me a firm grip. Our vicar, whose word we never doubted, said that a firm handshake was important! Consequently for many years I inflicted bone-crushing shakes on the congregation, unaware of the strength in my muscles, until a Christian banker in Paraguay told me that his hand had hurt all day on Monday from my handshake on Sunday!

Winter Saturdays were devoted to cutting and selling logs or catching rabbits. The summer was different. Hoeing long rows of mangel-wurzels could be backaching but a field cleaned from weeds looked good after several days' hard work. Haymaking and harvest brought its own satisfaction. I was 15 before I ploughed an acre in a day. This was the area expected of a proper ploughman, but unlike me the proper ploughmen didn't have to milk the cows as well.

In his old age my Uncle Ern commented on the way I, as a wiry 13 year old, could handle the manual tipping manure carts. We called these 'putts' in Somerset. They were gradually tilted to facilitate the unloading of the manure into heaps around the field, where it would continue to rot before spreading.

A test of ingenuity came when we switched from draught-horses to the Fordson tractor, which Dad bought when I was just 17. He also gave me his 1933 Austin Seven for my seventeenth birthday present. The mechanic from the Fordson agency lived in our village and he taught me much about reconditioning machines and keeping them in good mechanical order. Knowledge acquired then was invaluable for isolated travel in South America.

Early tractors were designed for towing tools, which were often adapted from horse-drawn implements. I discovered to my cost that unlike a horse, the tractor has no ears. I had dismounted to lift the harrows while they were still in motion. That was the easiest way to clean them, but I caught the harrow spike in my trouser turn-up and shouted 'whoa' in vain to the tractor. Luckily I did get free, and all was well. All would not have been well had the tractor gone through the hedge and across the main road, dragging me behind the harrow.

I sometimes get nostalgic about the old farm tools that we used. Most of these, like hay knives, pitchforks, sack hooks, three-legged stools, milkmaid yokes, horse rakes and carts, which have not rusted or rotted, now decorate pubs, or are to be found in museums. But no one who remembers the discomfort of feeding frozen turnips, or the icy water dripping down your back while cutting winter fodder called kale, will want those days back. Even the vibration and noise of the Fordson, with its unsilenced exhaust pipe a yard from the driver, has been replaced by warm, clean, computerized tractor cabs. The machine is more comfortable but the farmer is now more pressurized in the growing burden of control, meticulous planning and careful reporting.

The seeds of a missionary call

Fifty years ago the cultivation of the land often took precedence over the cultivation of the mind. My elders disapproved when the school leaving age was increased from 14 to 15. What else was there to learn anyway! Our little village school provided the basic education. The three lady teachers endeavoured to drum the three R's into us, and the first hour of the day was given to the fourth R, for religion. They were obviously Christians and taught religion with conviction and moral application. I later learnt that one of them was a devout Roman Catholic, which is why she taught me that Guy Fawkes was a good man, who was horribly tortured, along with the others, when his plans to get rid of a bad king failed. I thereby learned the most important lesson about history: there is more than one side to a story.

Granted that God always keeps a few surprises up his sleeve, if anyone had predicted that our one-street village would produce a bishop, most sensible people would not have put their bet on me! The more likely candidate would have been my best friend Victor Brown. He stimulated me academically and became a dedicated schoolteacher, in Africa and England. He never married and sadly died of cancer in his early forties.

A new grammar school, built two miles away on the road into Yeovil, looked a very attractive building and I had hoped to go there. But Victor was the only boy who went from our village school. Our headmistress had given him extra classes and she later told someone that she wished she had included others in these. I wished that I had been included.

Old Archdeacon Palmer was a godly, scholarly man who had been a Cambridge wrangler.[4] He tied his beard behind his neck while gardening, the same beard in which, according to mother, I entangled my fingers during my christening! Was that a prophetic or symbolic gesture? He probably felt depressed and isolated in the village congregation but he influenced me beyond measure by his example. I used to wander along to church and Mother remembered how at the age of eight I declared that I intended to be a missionary. A missionary call is not so much the impulse of a moment as the trend of a lifetime and Archdeacon Palmer set the trend even if I didn't understand his sermons. It was his posture and presence that preached the sermons, and that I could understand!

The archdeacon, who walked everywhere, died in a bleak war winter, after he had fallen off a high pavement. I wonder if he was depressed by the declining numbers, church debt and the terrible war clouds over Europe. I don't suppose that he imagined anyone like me would look back with such gratitude for the inspiration of his godly presence and demeanour. Curiously, years later I was ordained in Buenos Aires by his nephew, Bishop Daniel Ivor Evans, who although of a very different churchmanship had a warm spot for his uncle's protégé.

Our next vicar, Percy T. Norris, caused quite a stir. He claimed that his name Percy, a derivation of 'pierce eye', indicated that he should be a fighter, which he was. I am grateful for the evangelical convictions I learnt from P.T.N. but it took me a long time to appreciate the riches of other traditions. Thankfully his Protestantism was tempered by an evangelical fervour. Church suddenly became important to all of us. Little notices appeared around the village like, 'If everybody was just like me, what sort of church would our church be?' and 'I go to church on Sunday, not just the merest visit, so when at last I'm carried in, the Lord won't say, who is it?' The effect was summed up by our newly arrived policeman's wife, who said, 'I've never seen so much about church, it's a sin if you don't go!'

P.T.N.'s ministry watered the seeds sown by his predecessor. If one thinks of a moment of conversion I would put mine at the last day of January, 1943. I had been living with a mixture of guilt feelings and spiritual emotions not uncommon in a 14 year old. P.T.N. had announced that the Sunday afternoon service would be especially for young people. In those days that meant little more than some Scripture Union choruses instead of the third hymn in evening prayer. His sermon had, I remember, touched on dancing, which was frowned upon by evangelicals in those days, but he said we could dance if we did it for the glory of God, and not to do it otherwise! The crunch for me came when, in his inimitable way, he announced the last hymn, 'O Jesus, I have promised'. Half-way down the pulpit steps he stopped to exclaim, 'If you haven't promised, don't sing it!' There and then I made my silent promise, and experienced its initial outworking during the coming weeks.

There was much to learn. My commitment was to obedience in Christ's service. I had little understanding of the joy of forgiveness. Then I worried over whether I was believing properly! Christians have often been far too rigid in insisting that people come to faith in Christ through a rather stereotyped orthodox system, whereas as I read and re-read the gospels I am amazed by the way Jesus always met people on their own ground. He still meets us where we are so that we might journey on with him. To quote Rene Padilla, a South American theologian, 'Never make your expression into a precept, let God be as original with the rest as he has been with you.'

Archdeacon Palmer's memorial service included the switching on of new electric lights that, thanks to the new vicar, replaced the old brass oil lamps in the church. The sermon, on his outstanding missionary service in India, stirred up my sense of missionary calling but it seemed impossible that I could ever be a missionary. Then a few months later, at my confirmation, the Bishop of Taunton said, 'God has a purpose for your life. Your job is to find out that purpose and to fulfil it!' A few days later I was standing by the desk in the vicar's study, asking the question, 'Vicar, what do you think the chances are that I might become a missionary?'

'Bill', he said, 'if God has called you and your heart is in the right place, it is not a question of chance, it is a dead cert.'

The reply, so typical of Percy T. Norris, gave me new confidence, but it did not diminish my concern about the hurdles and difficulties, such as my lack of education. Even my meagre schooling up to 14 had been reduced by special wartime leave to dig up potatoes, etc. All children had little coupon books to indicate that they could be excused from school for several weeks to help work on the land. During my last year at school several of us covered exactly the same work in arithmetic as I had done when I was 12. I think it must have been that this was as far as the curriculum for primary education went in those days, leaving us and our parents with the impression that there was nothing else to learn about arithmetic. But the vicar said that if I wanted to be a missionary I should go to night school and learn English. He found country ways hard and grumbled about the noise of birds, so goodness knows what he thought of our Somerset dialect and grammar.

Youthful fervour

At 16 I became increasingly involved in Christian activity beyond our parish. Most of the Christians on my mother's side of the family were of Brethren persuasion, as were my friends in the branch of the National Young Life Campaign which met in Yeovil. Martin Cundy, a brilliant mathematician and father of the present Bishop of Peterborough, taught me that faith is not believing the ridiculous (such as 20 whales were about to be stranded outside the hall where we were meeting). True faith is not unreasonable, but it does take us beyond reason. All this provided fuel and furnace for my youthful fervour.

I wanted to preach and preach I did. We formed a preaching team and I wrote to chapels within 20 miles of us offering our services. A small chapel called Halfway House dated back to the seventeenth century. It was built half-way between Yeovil and Sherborne by the vicar of Yeovil when he was deposed by Elizabeth I's Act of Uniformity.[5] According to the old man who now ran the chapel, the small gallery window was a look-out point in case officers of the law came to apprehend the worshippers. He and his two sisters and some children they had befriended listened to my ill-prepared, but enthusiastic sermons.

The vicar's worst fears were realized when I asked him about adult baptism. I think he would have done well to treat my worries more lightly! Although I was eventually baptized by immersion in a Plymouth Brethren chapel I never doubted that I should remain in the local village church. It was to be several years before discussion and reading at All Nations Missionary College convinced me of the sound biblical, historical and pastoral reasons for the practice of infant baptism. I still have the Bible in which I had marked every verse I could find which related to the subject. Somehow those verses say something very different to me today. In fairness to my Brethren friends, who helped me more than I can say, it depends on the light in which we see baptism. The emphasis at that time was that we should be baptized in obedience to God, but being baptized is also recognition of what God has done and is doing in our children and us. The sacraments of baptism and holy communion are like precious diamonds. They reflect many different rays of truth. Sadly the Church has often quarrelled because of one-eyed emphasis upon one aspect of truth. And too often we have used the sacraments as instruments of discipline, whereas God has given them to us as instruments of mission for seekers in a needy world.

Sadly my premature and sometimes old-fashioned efforts, far from being effective, must often have made people wary. Like the occasion when an elderly evangelist persuaded me to don sandwich boards to advertise a local tent mission.

The vicar was anxious that I should offer myself for service with the BCMS (Bible Churchmen's Missionary Society) which was clearly evangelical. Their visiting speakers preached carefully prepared sermons, but I feared that I might become a cog in what seemed to be a rather precise wheel. Nor did I think that they would accept me as a missionary. In contrast, the Revd Norman Rutter, a SAMS (South American Missionary Society) deputation speaker, was not sensational. He preached the same low-key, but very sincere sermon on two successive visits (which may be why I remember bits of it!) and their literature actually said that they were looking for new missionaries. Dad, who now attended church, was also impressed by his sermon. He told of how missionaries had brought together three warring tribes at a place called La Paz on the banks of the Pilcomayo River, the very place where 20 years later I would take my first confirmation as a bishop!

Lifelong friends

P.T.N. felt, with reason, that I was dissipating my energies in extra parochial activities, but the long-term spin-off came in the formation of precious and influential lifelong friendships, particularly through the Young Life campaign and the Covenanter camps.

At 17, I spent my week's holiday at a Covenanter camp near Weymouth. There and at a subsequent camp in Ilfracombe I met three of my special friends: 'Skipper', the leader of the Covenanter movement, Ray Smith, an enthusiastic Christian teenager of my own age, and Tony Barratt, a veterinary surgeon.

'Skipper' (Captain Pinchbeck) treated me as an equal and a friend, in spite of my youth. He was a natural leader who had surprised himself by surviving the first war on the battlefields of France. He was the first Christian I met who courageously questioned the evangelical shibboleths, which we tended to accept in those days.

Through Ray Smith I was invited to speak at an evangelistic mission in the Brethren Hall in Woodford. They described me as 'the boy preacher from Somerset'. Ray and I kept in touch over the years, although our paths crossed only two or three times. He became a member of the

Church of England during his student days, while working with David Sheppard at the Mayflower Centre. I had hoped that he and his wife Gill could come to work in the Paraguay Chaco, where I thought his medical knowledge could be put to good use, but SAMS rightly sent them to Chile where they fulfilled an outstanding ministry in the English chaplaincy. Deafness hampered Ray's grasp of Spanish but did not prevent his natural communication, which brought Chileans and English people to faith in Christ.

My first meeting with Tony Barratt was very brief during the Covenanter camp in Ilfracombe. The campers visited St James' and St John's for evening prayer, which was well attended in those days. The service was often followed in evangelical churches with a short communion service, a lovely way to end the day for those who wished to stay after the vicar had said goodbye to the rest of the congregation at the door. During that brief period I chatted with Tony and formed a lasting impression, but neither of us imagined the influence we would have on each other's lives. Our paths next crossed when he moved as a new curate to Slough, and then ran parallel for many years in South America.

Notes

1   Named after the Collect for the Sunday before Advent, which began 'Stir up we beseech Thee O Lord'!
2   So called because it was sprung and lighter than heavy farm wagons. The driver sat up front. It served for light delivery work.
3   The Belgians had refused to extend the line along their border.
4   Which the dictionary defines as a student who is among the highest first-class honours achievers in Mathematics at Cambridge.
5   This can be found at the beginning of some 1662 Prayer Books.

2
TAPLOW

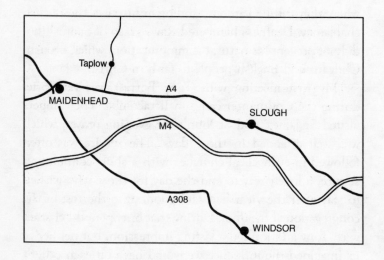

Greek under a haystack

It was October 1949 and I pushed my bicycle, with a large suitcase, up the hill from Taplow station to the All Nations Bible College.[1] (What a contrast to the car and trailer needed to take our Tim and his stuff to university almost 50 years later!)

All Nations College was a good choice. It had 40 students, a viable number for a theological college in those days. Most were in their late twenties and some had horrific wartime experiences behind them. My zest was an irritation to some of the more colourful characters and my rough and ready style seemed crude to those who came from a more urbane culture. Nor was it easy for me, a lively 19 year old, to change gear from the hyperactivity of the farm to the sedentary style of a student.

The college was governed strictly by the bell. We rose when it rang at 6 a.m. and, after half an hour for ablutions, we had an hour for private prayer and devotions, before chores at 7.30, breakfast at 8 a.m., chapel at 8.30 and lectures from 9 a.m. to 1 p.m. Four afternoons were given to technical training and gardening. I learnt photography, carpentry, building and book binding. There were prayers in the chapel after a heavy supper at 6 p.m. I once fell so soundly asleep on my knees that I only woke after it was all over, including the closing hymn. The students had wrapped a tablecloth around me! An older student took me aside and counselled against burning the midnight oil, which I tended to do by slipping away to the library after lights out at 10 or 10.30 p.m.

I was not alone in finding concentrated study difficult. It was so different from the tasks and smells of farming. Helpful books on the technique of reading and study were unheard of (even if they existed). It took me more than a week to master the first vocabulary in the most difficult Greek primer I have ever come across but on the Saturday afternoon, sitting under a haystack, I discovered that the words seemed to stay in my mind. From then on Greek words were pinned up in key places and tackled in odd moments.

It also seemed a good idea to study for 'matric', which was the equivalent of O levels in those days. I chose subjects where there was some overlap with the All Nations course, and enrolled on correspondence courses through Wolsey Hall, Oxford for some of the subjects. But one had to pass in all the subjects for matriculation and I ended up with a piece of paper saying that I had failed in the one subject which the college tutor thought I could do without the help of Wolsey Hall.

The students at All Nations were mostly from Church of England, Brethren and Baptist churches. I had rather naively felt that if I went abroad as a missionary I ought not to belong to any denomination because it was wrong to export divisions. My idealistic goal was just to take the Gospel, not a denomination. But how was this to be done? At that time, The Bible Society seemed to be the only organization which aimed at serving established churches overseas, rather than starting new ones, but it was very specialized.

Then one day our college principal, the Revd Brash Bonsall, pointed out, in one of his many asides, that the problem of denominations would not be solved by running away from them. 'If you don't go with a denomination', he said, 'you will end up starting your own.' Years later a wise Southern Baptist missionary said, 'Flagg, the best contribution you can make towards the unity of the church is to be a good Anglican.' I would see the truth of that many years later in Liverpool, where the church leaders made giant strides towards unity because they humbly knew where they stood themselves.

Some people unkindly described Brash Bonsall as an 'erratic eccentric'; but he appealed to me as a dynamic, unconventional man. His insatiable, magpie-like inquisitiveness enabled him to accumulate knowledge from many fields. His ideal for missionary candidates was that they should be 'jacks of all trades and masters of one'. He taught from a fundamentalist and legalistic stance, which some of us could not wholly share, even if we remained convinced of the trustworthiness of the Bible.

A challenge in Chile

Several of the students left to train for the Anglican ministry and I seriously considered approaching the Church of England selection board, but felt that I should first make further contact with SAMS (the South American Missionary Society).

My first letter, 18 months before, had not elicited a very encouraging response. This time, I received a very different reply from their new general secretary, Arthur Goodwin Hudson. He had recently returned from a chaplaincy in Chile, where he spent his holidays in the Araucanian mission. The previous SAMS general secretary had written to him explaining that he was about to retire and asked if he would consider the post. It was a good choice. Goodwin Hudson's decisive action (way ahead of the committee's discussion, let alone decision) was sorely needed. He changed the whole direction and ethos of the society which had been in terminal decline with an annual income of £16,000 and an expenditure of £18,000. In a matter of months, Goody (as he was known to his friends) had reduced the office staff (not without some pain) to two very capable secretaries, Miss Gooday and Miss Watker.

Miss Matthews, one of the former office staff, had previously served the society as a missionary in Chile. She told me how Goody had knocked her off balance one Monday morning as he nonchalantly sauntered into the office. 'Miss Matthews', he said, 'I've been thinking. Will you get out of the office and comb England!' That phrase described what she would do in an outstanding ministry of stirring up renewed interest in SAMS. Young people were enthused. One of them, Kathleen Clark (now the Revd Kath Lefroy), gave most of her life to outstanding service in SAMS, first as a missionary in Chile, then on SAMS home staff.

Goodwin Hudson stretched others and pushed himself to the limit with a remarkably effective ministry, first at St Mary Magdalene, Holloway Road, and then at All Saints, Woodford Green. At the same time he was director of the Billy Graham Evangelistic Association in the UK, the SAMS general secretary, and an evangelist with a roving ministry, often in the USA. He sometimes went straight from the Sunday evening service at Woodford Wells to Heathrow for a short mission in the States, returning in time for a Friday evening meeting at Woodford, hoping that the parish had not noticed his absence! An American bishop told me, 'I thank God for his transforming ministry in my life as a young priest.'

Goody did not like to commit himself too rigidly and was often as noncommittal as possible. He consulted reliable people before he interviewed anyone regarding a job. As a result, interviewees were often surprised when he offered them a post after the briefest of conversations. In my case, I learnt that he had consulted someone at All Nations before I received a reply to my letter. His secretary wrote that in view of my farming experience, the Revd Arthur Goodwin Hudson would like to talk to me about the possibility of my using this knowledge in Chile. Two weeks later, just before my twenty-second birthday, I was in the old SAMS office at 20 John Street, awaiting his arrival while his secretary, Susan Gooday, was 'damming' the ancient typewriter because it had run away with itself!

Goodwin Hudson, who always seemed casual, sauntered in flashing his silk scarf and gold cufflinks. He was always dapper, but I did just wonder if he had been drinking! He asked if I could wait while he sorted out one or two things, thus giving me a few helpful, but nervous moments between meeting him and sitting at his desk. He called me in, apologized for his dilapidated office (which looked all right to me) and rapidly set me at ease by his friendly, straight-to-the-point conversation.

He wanted people with a 'Pauline vision', meaning that like the Apostle Paul he wanted me to earn my way. 'Worthwhile people should be able to do two or three jobs.' He was looking for 'people with the ability to take the initiative, so that if the church lacked decent hymn-books they would make sure it got some'. Forty-seven years on I can still remember the challenge as he presented it. A mission farm in Chile would soon be without an administrator. Would I be willing to postpone my plans in order to take charge of the farm and work as an evangelist? Otherwise SAMS would pigeon-hole my letter while I went to a theological seminary to train for ordination. 'But', he said, 'make sure that the seminary doesn't become a cemetery . . . too many go in alive and come out dead.' The vitality of his conversation stays with me today. He was a man who knew where he was going and that he wanted me to make the most of my life for God.

Others would have given more careful answers to my questions. I explained that I was about to become engaged. He thought that it would be possible for me to save up enough money to return to England in 1952 or 1953 to marry Marj, after I had spent a couple of years preparing the way. He didn't mention that the probationary missionary pay at that time was £175 a year, rising to £200 after 24 months! It seemed prudent to keep my questions short because he was fingering an unopened airmail envelope and seemed worried about what it might contain. How long would I have to make up my mind? 'A week or so.' If I said yes, when would the society want me to go? 'The boat usually sails around September!'

Back at college the students were even more astounded than I was. I talked to Brash Bonsall, who encouraged me to get to Chile, 'before we are all blown up by an atomic bomb here'. That was not a good motive even if he, like many others at that time, was understandably obsessed by the danger of the Cold War and the conflict in Korea. He gave me permission to go down to Somerset over the weekend to talk about this with my parents and with Marj, my fiancée-to-be. In our quasi-monastic set-up, we were not normally given time away during term-time!

A unique romance

My friendship with Marj had blossomed into love and this was to be the first of many times when she would give me completely unselfish support. Before I met her I felt that if I was to become a missionary I ought not to think about getting married. Mother had been concerned about this and she and Dad were very pleased when Marj came on to the scene.

Our courtship followed a unique pattern. Beauty was in the eye of the beholder when Marj saw me in the choir at church and was attracted by the back of my neck! She had come south for a practical course in domestic science at the nearby village of Chilton Cantelo. My first approach to her was to ask if she could encourage a number of girls from the training centre to attend an evangelistic rally for which we were hiring a bus. Not long after that, on one of her days off, she happened to be near a field gate just outside of Mudford, and I stopped the tractor to give her a ride around the field I was rolling and harrowing. Before long I was taking her home after church and we often cycled the 15 miles to the large home where she later worked in Wincanton.

The unselfish way in which she responded so positively to the challenge of this opportunity was a great encouragement. My parents were understandably concerned and I now realize how much they must have worried about me.

Not many missionary societies today would send a 22 year old with so little experience into the situation that existed in Chile. The SAMS selection procedure for new missionaries was fairly basic at that time, but they were to send some outstanding people, thanks to the judgement of Goody Hudson and his successor, Harry Sutton.

I was called to the society's committee, which met monthly, but they were too busy with other matters to see me, so I was interviewed by a dear old clergyman called Anderson. He had two questions. The first was used regularly by Bishop Taylor Smith when appointing chaplains for the First World War: 'If you knew that a man had five minutes to live, what would you tell him?' The second was whether I was inclined towards what he referred to as the theological stance of the CMS (Church Missionary Society), or that of the BCMS (Bible Churchmen's

Missionary Society). The BCMS had split from CMS on a commitment to apply much more rigid guidelines on the theological position of their missionaries.

Those two questions homed in on the heart of the Gospel and my basic theological convictions and attitude. I said that anyone with five minutes to live did not need to be told about his or her sins. They needed to be told about a loving Saviour and Lord who was ready to forgive them. On the second question, I responded that while I was a convinced evangelical I wanted to work in an open struc- ture. At that time SAMS did not have a basis of faith, but insisted that its missionaries should be confirmed mem- bers of the Church of England. I still do not believe that making people sign over-defined statements defends orthodoxy. God's truth is too big for that and must be lived and proclaimed. When Spurgeon, the great Baptist preacher, was asked why he didn't do more to defend the Bible, he replied, 'Whoever heard of anyone defending a lion?'

During the summer, Marj and I talked about where she might obtain missionary preparation and we decided on Mount Hermon Missionary Training College. In retro- spect, this was not the best choice for a girl with a fair measure of independent judgement who did not easily conform to all the narrow shibboleths. On one occasion she was wrongly rebuked for not wearing stockings. It seems that the ones she had on did not have seams, so that it could not be seen that she was wearing them! She still does not know what that has to do with the Gospel! But when Mount Hermon and All Nations merged, the mixed college built on all that was good in their traditions.

Marj's independence and unwillingness to toe rigid

lines in every issue has been good for me. Without her, I think I could have been an unbearable prig. (To which my daughter Ros responds, 'No you wouldn't, Dad, you would have just been an eccentric 40 years ago instead of waiting till now!') I am sure that the history of my first two years in Chile would have been very much more positive had I been able to share the benefit of Marj's judgement. But who knows? We were both rather young to get married, so we waited faithfully for each other in very different worlds. We learnt a few lessons along the way and, under the goodness of God, things eventually came right!

Note

1 Previously All Nations Bible College, now All Nations Christian College.

3
CHILE

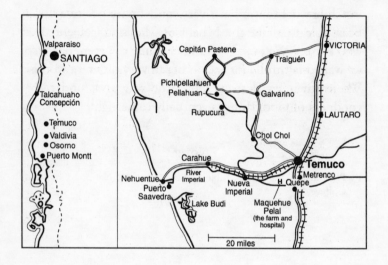

Leaving home

Early on Thursday morning [3 October] ... a party of
friends met at Euston Station to see him [Bill Flagg]
off on his long journey. The Rev C. W. Anderson led
in prayer on the station platform committing Mr
Flagg to the Lord. Then amidst all the farewells he
boarded the train, which carried him to ... embark
on *La Reina* for his month's voyage.

(SAMS magazine 1951)

I had left home the previous day. Dad, who could not

bring himself to say goodbye, had gone out early. Mother stood by my side as I almost burst the holdall she had thoughtfully given me to push in last-minute things. I was conscious of their heartache, but as a young 22 year old I was excited at leaving England on a lifetime commitment. It was my moment in mission. Neither they nor my fiancée Marj at Mount Hermon Missionary Training College could share the excitement. The boat train steamed non-stop from Euston, to *La Reina del Pacifico* in the Liverpool dock where I handed in my wartime ration book and identity certificate before boarding.

Captain Dex, a long-serving Salvation Army officer, took me under his wing and taught me much, including some Spanish, during the following four sometimes seasick weeks. He had expected to knock the world over (with God's help of course) and he was discouraged because none of the exciting things described in missionary magazines seemed to happen. But, said he, 'You need to look back and you will see that those things do happen. They have to be set in the context of disappointment, discouragement, misunderstanding and struggles with the language and faithful service!'

Like most of my generation I had never been overseas so the boat journey helped me to prepare for a different way of life. In Cherbourg I saw armed policemen for the first time. Cuba's Havana in pre-Castro, pre-Communist days, left lasting memories of extrovert people and the fervent singing of the Spanish translations of Moody and Sankey hymns. I saw real destitution in Cartagena, Venezuela. Some passengers criticized the nuns coming aboard to collect left-over food from the ship's galley for their orphanage. They would have done better to think of the plight of orphans living from the dustbins and garbage dumps of the Third World.

On our last Sunday we had an overnight stop at Callao, 15 miles west of Lima. It was the Feast of the Christ of the Miracles.[1] Pilgrims crowded the streets and the smell of incense from the chanting processions mingled with that of richly spiced food being cooked on pavement barbecues. A rather fat lady was swooning in the crowd. Everyone seemed to be in a highly emotional and sometimes almost zombie-like state. I felt that if ever missionaries were needed they were needed there, where to my English mind so much needed changing![2]

Mr Milbourne, the mission superintendent, met me in Valparaiso and we travelled by train via Santiago, the capital, then south to Temuco. The dormer coach did not have separate compartments but the facing seats were let down, while the upper bed was pulled out. Heavy curtains provided privacy. The expected arrival time of the daily train service would be reported on the local radio and we were in Temuco on time at 2 p.m. next day.

First days at the farm

A cloud hung over my early days in Chile. The mission had gone through years of retrenchment. The post-war devaluation of the pound meant that SAMS could no longer subsidize all the philanthropic institutions. I arrived when the financial situation had worsened further and I allowed myself to be infected with a critical negative attitude of what had gone before.

Winston Churchill once said, 'Any fool can tell me what's wrong, I want someone to tell me what's right.'

There was, however, still a lot that was right in Chile. The boys' and girls' boarding schools in the small town of Cholchol continued to flourish, as did the rural schools, which also served as churches across the region. The rural ministry had its champion in the indomitable 'Struggles' who, years later at the age of 90, decided that she was too old to ride horseback to the country churches and persuaded a Mapuche lad to take her everywhere on the back of his motorcycle. Baptized Eleanor Strugnel, she was so small at birth that the doctor said, 'Put her in a shoebox, she won't live.' She defied him and others for 106 years until her death in May 1993.[3] Late in life she married Canon William Wilson, who came out of retirement to join her in caravan evangelism.

'Daddy' Wilson was deaf and almost blind as I sat on the edge of his bed and asked him about the start of the mission in 1894, when he had written, 'It is now some three or four weeks since I landed in Chile. I shall like both the country and the people very well . . . We must devote all our energies to getting hold of their own language . . . I am thankful that the Lord has given us such a man as Mr Sadleir to be our leader and still more thankful to think that I serve the Lord Christ.' Before his conversion and call to the ministry, Charles Sadleir had been a politician in Manitoba, so he was well able to press the Mapuche land rights at the highest levels of the Chilean government. He became the main speaker at all the Mapuche gatherings (called concentrations) and their chiefs showed their gratitude by giving him land on the banks of the river Quepe where he and a fellow Canadian moved once the mission was established in Cholchol.

Then he acquired an adjacent 500 acres. This farm

became the centre for his future ministry. Two converted Indian chiefs stayed at his home for months on end as they helped him in the first translation of the New Testament into Mapudungo (the tongue of the land). He established large boarding schools for primary education and vocational training on the land he acquired for the mission. In retrospect I feel, however, that the acquisition of the extra 500 acres was a mistake. Just enough land for the educational institution would have been fine and the possession of a small farm, Allihuen, as a gift from the Mapuche chiefs was a great honour. The purchase of more land from the Chileans, whose ancestors had at some stage stolen it from the indigenous people, bred resentment in the later years. Moreover, for legal reasons Sadleir could only purchase the land in his own name and that caused a major conflict with his then bishop.

After Sadleir left, the mission had great difficulty finding the right farm managers and for a while the farm was rented. It seemed to be contributing little to the mission when I was given the challenge of doing something with it and rather like Charles Sadleir I threw myself into doing everything I could.

The traditional method was to sow grain (wheat or oats) one year and leave the land fallow for two. But there was scope for better crop rotations. Potatoes paid off prior to sowing wheat, especially when we could purchase guano from the north.[4] We despatched our first ten tons of potatoes by rail to Antofagasta. Sugar beet, although not as profitable as potatoes, ensured a good wheat harvest, at little cultivation cost, the subsequent year. I got the mill working round the clock for the benefit of our neighbours, and the bran we received as payment was used to feed pigs which we bought in from local Mapuches for fattening. Harvests vacillated from glut to scarcity almost annually. If there was a scarcity, say, of oats, prices were high and everyone would sow oats for the next year, and when prices dropped because of the glut no one would sow oats the following year. It didn't take much intuition to do the opposite and sow the crop that was currently overproduced. We planted the less fertile and inaccessible corners of the farm with thousands of young trees that could be culled and eventually harvested to yield more profit per acre than any other crop, if one did not mind waiting 20 years!

Our endeavours were not without setbacks and near misses, like foot and mouth disease. The worst problem was the loss of most of our wheat harvest in the year when I took advantage of the government's interest-free loans for the purchase of fertilizers. The appearance of the wheat deluded me into expecting a bumper harvest. Instead, the combine harvester produced nothing but chaff due to a spring frost that had struck at the critical pollination moment.

People seemed to trust me as patron, probably because there was no one else locally in a similar position. Some couples brought their marriage disputes, ranging from the serious to the relatively light-hearted. A wife turned up to say that she had been beaten up and showed me her arms, which she said would be 'black and blue by tomorrow'. The situation seemed serious until her husband arrived in a penitent mood and harmony was restored.

Two Mapuche neighbours appealed to me because they had fallen out over the borders of their land. These misunderstandings could arise where there were no proper

fences and I knew what Moses was talking about in the
Old Testament when he said, 'Thou shalt not remove thy
neighbour's land mark.'[5] One of the antagonists had ridden
off to the nearest judge in the little railway town of Quepe
and now they were both summoned to court. They asked
if I could intervene to stop the case, so the next day the
three of us rode to Quepe to see the judge. They were both
contrite and had come to an understanding, but the judge,
who I think was slightly amused, was reluctant to let them
off. He agreed to reduce the charge of bodily harm (it
wasn't too grievous) to one of an altercation with the use
of foul language, for which they both had to pay a fine of
about two days' wages.

A reputation for hard riding

It was said of William Haslam, a nineteenth-century church
building parson, that he, his horse and his dog were the
three thinnest creatures in Cornwall. My two horses were
well fed and I didn't have a dog, but I drove myself hard
enough to keep thin. Unwittingly I built up a reputation for
hard riding. It would take me 20 minutes to gallop cross-
country to Metrenco, where I would get the train, after
stabling the horse with a local engineer called Bolemey.
One day the train was just pulling out of the station. I
threw the reins over the railway fence, in sight of Bolemey,
who gave me the thumbs up. As I scrambled through the
railway fence, the driver spotted me and slowed down
enough for me to jump on to the steps of the Wild West-
type coach. I enjoyed the episode, but that evening the local
schoolteacher at Metrenco, a dynamic young lady, con-
fronted me on my return with the words, 'I've heard about

your hard riding and I shall report you to the society for the prevention of cruelty to animals.' To which I could only reply, 'I have never worn spurs, I never use a whip and if my horse shows signs of ill treatment you must report me.' It was a good answer, and she accepted it, but I was humbled by the confrontation. Spurs and whips were generally used to excess by too many riders and I discouraged them on the farm. I sometimes rode with a loose rein on long journeys while I tried to emulate John Wesley by reading in the saddle![6] But when I was in a hurry all I needed to do was to run the back of my hand up the horse's mane. Either of my two horses would then take off at an all-out gallop and the one that was blind in one eye would half turn its head for maximum vision.

As I rode along the tracks of the undulating country-side I could usually see between six and 12 Mapuche homesteads. The thatched roofs of the older homes, called rucas, came right down to the ground. The smoke from the fire on the ground, where all the cooking took place, escaped through a small opening under the eaves and cracks in the roof. Little babies were comfortably cushioned with wool and tied on to a specially carved wide wooden plank, which in fine weather stood upright outside the ruca.

There was something idyllic about riding up to their houses and waiting in the saddle until invited to dismount. To set foot on the land before such an invitation would be akin to entering a stranger's home uninvited in England. It was always a joy to visit Manuel Llancavil, a lively charismatic teacher and pastor. He was full of encouragement, especially to the group of young men who were to become future church leaders in the area. He was a successful farmer who sometimes still threshed the wheat in the traditional method of trotting horses around a gradually diminishing pile as their hooves beat out the grain. Once I took the caravan to his farm with the tractor and ploughed one of his fields, holding evangelistic meetings in the evenings, but I usually stayed in his home, apart from short visits for Sunday services.

The mission boarding schools had educated and established Manuel and other brighter pupils as rural schoolteachers. The Chilean government eventually paid them but the mission still helped with loans, as the annual 'subvention', as it was known, was often 12 months late. The schoolrooms were built of rough sawn timber planks, with galvanized iron roofs. On wet days the pungent smell of clothes drying around the wood-burning stove mingled with the body odours of about 40 children. It rained a lot in wintertime! On Sunday the building became a chapel and the teacher was often the preacher.

A view over Cholchol

When the small medical dispensary on the farm was destroyed by fire we converted a mission bungalow into a cottage hospital, run mainly for tuberculosis patients by Nurse Helen Bridge. That developed into an important state recognized medical centre. The other mission hospital, which also served a vast area, had been established and run in the town centre of Cholchol by the formidable Dorothy Royce. During the Independence Day celebrations the locals invented a cruel game of hanging a goose upside down over an old oil drum. The first galloping horseman to jump the drum and grab the goose's neck could take it home. Miss Royce objected to the local mayor about the cruelty of the sport. He responded, 'Senorita Royce, I can do nothing.' She decided that she could and would do something. She marched across the field, sat firmly on the barrel under the goose and said, 'Right! The next person to jump will jump over me! I am here until that goose is taken down.' Nobody would dare jump over Miss Royce anywhere let alone on a barrel! The fact that she had recently received Chile's highest award to a foreigner, the Bernardo O Higgins medal, for her service, added extra authority.

The Cholchol mission pump house had burned down soon after my arrival in Chile. People expected me to have enough know-how to put it right and, as usual, the challenge stretched my capacity! Rebuilding the pump house itself was fairly straightforward. But the fire had damaged the tower above and I felt like an amateur steeplejack as I climbed the iron fittings to the top of the tank. Once up and safely inside the concrete tank I surveyed a vast area. Below me Cholchol, a little town of just over a thousand people, was laid out in a grid system. There were no paved roads. Horses were hitched up outside the local store. A bullock cart followed the ruts on one side of the wide avenue as its owner brought a sack of wheat in for milling. The only 'public transport' was a lorry which, when the earth roads were dry in summertime, went into the provincial capital of Temuco once a week. Its paying passengers were crowded on top of its other cargo. This whole area for an all too brief period would be the scene of some of our happiest ministry in our final year in Chile.

The following weekend I did one of the most useful things in my life. Maud Bedwell, one of the four lady missionaries, and I talked rather gloomily about the fact that the appointment of the Revd Peter Tadman to a chaplaincy would leave us without an ordained missionary. I mentioned that I knew a curate, Tony Barratt, who had been a veterinary surgeon, and we agreed that I should ask him if he could join us.[7] I wrote that evening, and just over a week later Tony, who had been praying for guidance about his next sphere of service, rose from his knees to pick up my letter in the morning post. He responded positively, and following consultation with SAMS it was not long before we knew that he and his family would be on their way. Soon after his arrival he urged Douglas Milmine, his fellow curate at Slough, to join us. It was not easy for Doug and Ros to respond. Their fifth baby, Stephen, had lived for only three days. They made a tentative offer for a short period of service, but continued within SAMS until their retirement.

Marriage and malleability

Marj completed her missionary training and came to join me in Chile. Everyone was expecting us to set a wedding date fairly quickly, but she had doubts and our engagement was temporarily broken on Christmas Day 1953. That actually helped, and when she later moved to Cholchol, the rebuilding of our relationship was pretty rapid. Once re-engaged neither of us wanted to hang around, so 4 May 1954 was the day set for our church wedding. The civil ceremony took place on 3 May, when an admonition of the duties of partners to each other was followed by a short affirmation from us that we wanted to be married. We were then asked how many children we wanted to legalize. This was a surprising question; at that time we were not used to the idea of couples living together and producing children before their marriage. It was, however, evidently normal in Chile, because the wedding certificate, issued in the form of a book, contained a section for the legitimizing of children born prior to the marriage. There were also pages for registering subsequent births!

Meanwhile, back at the mission Ros Milmine and Nurse Muriel Parrott were working hard to prepare a wedding reception. The local schoolmaster and farm-workers who arranged the open-air stew and barbecue said that the proper thing for me to do as farm manager would be to provide an ox for roasting. Five sheep were more in line with our budget and actually provided more meat than a single bullock. This was needed when it seemed that all the neighbours had invited themselves. The Chilean meal of soup and barbecued mutton was stretched, but no one complained. There was a mixture of nationalities at the wedding, with English and Spanish used at the service and reception. As the horses towed us from the church through the orchard to the bungalow the schoolchildren sang an old chorus, 'With Jesus in the family, what a happy home', in Mapuche, Spanish and English.

In those days, the acme of missionary service was to spend the whole of one's life in the same place. Canon 'Daddy' Wilson interjected strongly, 'They *must* stay all their lives', when one speaker expressed the hope that we would stay there many years! That was our intention, as we returned from our honeymoon to the large, well-built wooden farmhouse. Little did we realize that in the next 16 years we would make our home in at least 16 houses. We did not of course have as many different postings, but starting new work in new areas often involved renting the first thing we could find for a while, then moving on to something more suitable, then purchasing or building, once the plans were formalized. Ours was a secure but not very settled existence! Like most couples, we had our moments! I am not given to delay and I did not spend enough time in consultation. My mother was a submissive person. Thank God I had married a very supportive but not a submissive wife!

We were looking forward to a family. Marj had told my dad that she hoped to have six children and we said that perhaps after producing our own, God willing we might also adopt. One of the poorer ladies who had a large family brought her latest to Marj and asked if we could adopt her. This did not seem to be the right thing to do, although we later cared for a desperately neglected baby in Cholchol. Little Rosita was born of a crippled lady, who spent all her time in a wheelchair. Nobody admitted knowing how she had become pregnant, but it was almost certainly a case of incest, if not rape. While we were able to look after Rosita she put on weight and the awful smell from lack of washing gradually diminished. Sadly we had to give her back to her mother as our home leave approached and it wasn't long before we heard that she had died. The plight of babies like Rosita caused us to think about an orphanage.

Meanwhile, our first baby, Richenda, arrived. Nurse Helen Bridge responded positively to our request to attend to the delivery at home. Shendy, as she became known, was only ten days late, but after successful inducement the birth was a long and frightening story. Labour started at about 11 p.m. and Helen was with Marj upstairs. In those days, the husband was expected to stay downstairs and provide lots of hot water and wait. I waited and waited and at 6 a.m. Helen came downstairs very worried to say that the delivery was difficult and she felt we should go into Temuco, 25 miles away. We had a truck on loan from the Milmines, but it was out of order because I had been unable to obtain the spare parts. Mercifully, the precarious telephone line was operational and unusually the erratic lady in charge of the small exchange system actually responded at 7 a.m. and got me through to Doug Milmine in Temuco. Doug and Ros came out immediately in their Land Rover, arriving soon after 8 a.m. We put Marj on an improvised stretcher made of a short ladder with a horse-hair mattress. The assembled farm-workers looked very worried as we carried her out to the Land Rover. That anxious time engraved upon my mind the meaning of the Prayer Book litany, 'that it may please Thee to pre-serve . . . all women labouring of child . . . we beseech Thee to hear us good Lord.'

I concentrated on keeping up maximum speed while avoiding as many of the potholes in the gravel road as possible and we arrived at the doctor's clinic soon after 10 a.m., to find that he had several deliveries on his hands. Marj spent another hour on her improvised stretcher on the floor of his waiting room with the doctor occasionally listening to the baby's heart. He kept promising that the delivery room would soon be free and it was a relief when she eventually went in. It seemed only a short time before I was called in to see our beautiful baby. We named her Richenda, a Romany name meaning a fighter, and Elizabeth, meaning God promises to keep his promises. We returned to the farm and the nursery room that Marj had painted

and prepared during her pregnancy, but we were there for
only a few months before we moved over to Cholchol.

Renewal in Auracania

I wrote a despondent letter in 1954. It seemed as if most
of the rural schools cum churches were moribund. Even
the mission church on the farm was poorly attended.
Apart from the help of an aged Chilean lay reader, the
church work seemed to depend upon a few missionaries.
Several of us agreed to rise early every Wednesday morning
to pray for revival. No one was likely to disturb us at 5 a.m.
because Chile lives late! We rightly believed that prayer
would bring change, because good things come about
when people choose to join their small tributaries of
prayer to the mighty river of God's will. Seeds of hope
began to sprout through a growing interest among the
farm-workers.

I invited a Mapuche evangelist called Luis Nahuelpan
for a week's mission on the farm and 30 of the workers
listened to his simple and effective explanation of the
Gospel in the farmhouse each evening. Were they attending
just to please me as the boss? I think not, because their
interest permeated from them to the neighbourhood and
they suggested that we ask Tony Barratt and Florencio, a
Chilean evangelist, to conduct a mission in our little
church. This resulted in a number becoming active
Christians.

The work in Cholchol and the surrounding area came
alive under Tony's ministry. The leadership of the rural
churches was strengthened through a monthly day conference for teachers and evangelists.[8] This led on to an

inspirational weekend conference for the entire region. It was a real watershed. Several retired missionaries who had pioneered the work made their voices heard, including one of the mission founders, Canon 'Daddy' Wilson who, because of frailty, had sent in written contributions. Nevertheless he struggled to his feet to participate for the last time in his life in a public meeting. The people clung reverently to the old man's words: 'I have worked here in Araucania for 60 years now and my desire has always been to see the national Church established and served, by capable and consecrated men and women, enthusiastic in the work of Christ. This is what we are seeing now and I say, Glory, glory, alleluia to the Lord.'[9]

We were young people, left to get on with the job! During my six years we had only one visitor, the treasurer from the SAMS committee in London; and two visits from our Bishop who was based on the other side of the continent in Buenos Aires.

Reg Bartle, a fervent curate from London, brought the SAMS missionary staff up to three clergy, one layman (myself) plus our wives and four single lady missionaries. Reg, an ex-army engineer, planned his days with meticulous timing and usually kept to his plan even in South America. I fixed up a small flat for him, his wife Thelma with their infant son Mark in what had once been the boarding school. It was also my job to teach Reg to ride a horse and introduce him to the area. He was understandably frustrated on our first visit to a rural school because his nag needed pushing and he pressed me to change horses for our return journey. I did warn him that his horse was safe, but that mine 'would go'! We had just turned towards home when I got the old nag he had been riding, to canter.

It was then that I heard the thud, thud and thud, of Reg's mount galloping up behind me. It tore past us in a dry ditch, perilously close to the thorny hedge, before Reg's hat flew off and he disappeared into a cloud of dust. But where others would have fallen he somehow managed to hold on with typical tenacity and stop his steed with its nose in the hedge.

We were well fed on our rural visits but some local dishes were not attractive to the unaccustomed visitor. I never brought myself to enjoy horsemeat, which tasted sweeter than beef and was often served up on special occasions, particularly at funerals. When Reg first attended the burial of a Mapuche Indian he was offered a meal of 'sopaipillas' (a sort of bread doughnut) cooked in the fat of the deceased's horse, which, in accordance with custom, had been slaughtered for the funeral feast. One rancid bit was enough! Not to cause offence, he slipped the remaining pieces one by one into his wellington boots when his host was not looking. From that moment, he had half a dozen dogs around his legs. They stuck by him even when he had mounted his horse for the return journey. Only when he was at a discreet distance from the house, could he empty his wellingtons and leave the dogs to enjoy the stuff.

The Mapuches baked delicious bread in the ashes of the fire on the ground. Cazuela, a watery chicken stew with potatoes, was enriched by the crushed end of red hot pepper. Weevils often hatched and tunnelled out in the dried peas and beans, and when these floated to the top of the stew they were usually skimmed off before serving. I was once in the home of a widower where this did not happen, however. I ate what I could and it was a relief when he left the room and I could skim off and dispose of the remainder of the weevils through cracks in the rough wooden floor.

A last year in Cholchol

By 1956 I had spent five years in Chile and was due for home leave, but as Marj had served only three we balanced out the difference. This enabled us to replace the Barratts for a year in Cholchol while they were on leave in England. I also continued to have the oversight of the farm, which was run by a Chilean foreman.

Marj was very patient over the change in our plans. Baby Richenda had hardly slept in her newly painted bedroom before our possessions were loaded on to the tractor trailer and we perched ourselves in comfortable chairs on the back of it for the four-hour journey via Temuco to Cholchol. I had my long fishing rod available so that I could just reach over our stuff to touch Fermin, the tractor driver, if we wanted him to stop. Unfortunately, half-way there I dropped the rod and jumped down to rescue it. For all my running the tractor was faster! A long walk for me and a disturbing journey for Marj would have ensued had there not been a bend in the road a quarter of a mile on and Fermin looked back over the open countryside to see me plodding and waving!

Our home in Cholchol was in a wing of the U-shaped school, which had first-floor boarding facilities for boys. There were lots of fleas in the south of Chile and we were the only edible residents left when the boarders went home for the school holidays! Marj had made a straw mattress to fit our bed. It was very comfortable, but we discovered to our cost that it also provided an ideal home for hungry fleas. Years later when some of our goods caught us up in Paraguay she was quite sentimental about one dead flea which she found in a blanket! Just a little bit of Chile!

Tony Barratt had carefully managed the mission finances and he instructed me to use the cash in hand to repair and restore our dilapidated buildings. Among other problems the wooden blocks, which supported the Cholchol church, had rotted. The wooden floor had an interesting rise and fall and the walls were subsiding. We squeezed underneath the building and gradually lifted the structure with several old-fashioned car and lorry jacks before pouring concrete into new moulds for foundation blocks.

My one deep regret is that with so many things happening I failed woefully in my ministry to my own wife, particularly when Marj suffered a miscarriage later in the year. In keeping with the then missionary atmosphere of the stiff upper lip I was encouraged to continue my working programme in Cholchol for a week while she was in Temuco, being carefully cared for by Doug and Ros Milmine.

Marj later told me how worried she used to be when most weeks I would ride off, with my saddlebags behind me, for three-day tours on a very lively horse. Mercifully I was not thrown too often but there was one frustrating experience when, after several days away, I was within half an hour of home and had to cross just one more river. The ferry had a simple DIY system. If it had been left on the other side of the river it could be pulled back by an attached rope and the rope from the other side would be used to pull oneself across. I dismounted, but didn't hitch up the reins, and was about to pull the ferry into the river when the horse (which like me was hungry) decided to jump off and eat the succulent new wheat shoots in a near-by field. For almost two hours he played the game of eat and run just far enough to give himself space for another munch. Eventually I caught the brute when he had had his fill, and I was hungrier! This time he was firmly hitched before I tugged my way across the river.

Our last winter in Chile was very severe. It was stimulating to ride into the storm on a dark night, dressed as I was in the black cloak (called a manta castilla) and a tight fitting broad-rimmed hat. But the persistent cold rain killed many of our neighbour's animals and following a poor crop a lot of people consumed all their wheat several months before the next harvest. Wheat or flour was available on credit at an inflated price so that at harvest time two bags would have to be sold to pay the cost of one which had been purchased in the bleak winter and early spring.

I talked with Doug and the local church leaders in Cholchol about the possibility of setting aside a fund to purchase flour which could be loaned to some poverty-stricken families until the harvest, three months on. Since those days, thank God, huge amounts of money have been given through relief organizations like Oxfam, Tear Fund and Christian Aid. In comparison, our little efforts were paltry, but the 'drop in the ocean' helped some.

I left before repayment was due and often wondered how that had worked out and, indeed, whether it would be felt that we had misused mission funds. It was a relief years later to read a report by Barbara Bazley, the bishop's wife, that the church members continued to 'put away part of their harvest against the winter months, making it available at its original price once local supplies were exhausted. The proceeds would still be given to the pastors' fund but without profiteering and as a service to the less privileged.'

A living church

It was the care of the living church that thrilled me most. Some members of the church in Cholchol met early on Sunday mornings to pray before the missionaries and local evangelists set out from the mission compound for occasional visits to the little rural churches. We worked out the rota and had to ensure that the half-dozen horses were shod and well fed for the journeys.

Tony Barratt had particularly asked me to encourage Panguilef Loncomil, a teenage Christian. He had almost died of tuberculosis, but he found healing in body and soul in the mission hospital. His relatives were pleased to have him back, but not pleased by his newfound faith. Yet, in spite of their opposition, he was able to start services in the local school building and I arranged to go there for a meeting. He explained that because of his parents' antagonism he would not be able to offer me accommodation so I slept on the benches in the little school. It was a cold night and in the early morning moonlight I saw Pangui outside his home in the valley, looking up to see if I was all right! Twenty years later, he, as a university professor, would give me the place of honour at a meal to celebrate the graduation of his eldest son from primary school. The boy went on to obtain the first place in the national university entrance examinations in chemistry. It was Pangui's own desire for further learning that moved us to get access for him and several others into secondary education. They spent some weeks in Cholchol, where I was able to arrange tuition. They were not successful that year, but with the help of other missionaries they kept at it. Some became church leaders and Pangui, who was not ordained, became a wonderful man of encouragement and counsel across the future diocese. He served for 25 years as general secretary of the Diocesan Executive Council and played a crucial role in the development of the diocesan education work, including a school for deaf people in Temuco, before he died in his forties.

Following that cold night I continued my journey from Pangui's to an area called Pellahuen. It was mostly uphill and towards the end we had to cross a fast-flowing river in a canoe carved out of a tree trunk. My horse swam behind as I held on to the reins. Half-way across I asked if it was safe and, answering for the boat and not the passenger, the oarsman replied, 'Yes, we lost a sack of wheat last week but the boat didn't sink.' Then he paddled around to point out the burst bag of wheat at the bottom of the clear river!

Domingo Cayuman, an impressive man, and his brother Segundo had founded a little church at Pellahuen, about a mile up the other side of the river. Someone had given Domingo a copy of Matthew's gospel when they met briefly on one of the river ferries. He was convinced and converted by its message, as was his brother, and they visited the mission in Cholchol to learn more, while starting meetings amongst their family and friends. Domingo was very anxious that we should visit the nearest small town, called Pichi (meaning little) Pellahuen, which he rightly said needed the Gospel!

Doug Milmine accompanied me on my next visit and we rode up to the one-street place of Pichi. It could have been the setting for a cowboy film. We made contact with a butcher, who seemed to have the most prosperous business apart from the cantinas (local bars). He and his wife agreed to give me accommodation at a reasonable price, and he said that he would invite his neighbours to hear the message in the big room behind the shop. A month later I was back again for a weekend. We seemed to get on well. Too well, I thought, when he turned to his wife and said, 'He's all right, we don't need to clear out another room, he can sleep with us.' It was a relief that 'with us' only meant 'in our room', as they had an extra bed, under an impressive crucifix, where I slept like a log. It had been a long day, with the horse ride, visits to key people and an unusual evening service. The cantinas did a great trade on Sundays and their tipsy clients were all interested in what I might have to say. The butcher guarded his door and would let in only those who were reasonably sober. There was enough shouting outside to make me thankful for his vigilance.

I would remember that event on another occasion in Paraguay, when I was conducting a service on someone's patio. I had just closed my eyes and started the Lord's Prayer, when a drunk, who until then had shown no signs of being the worse for wear, let out a yell and simultaneously punched me under my nose. It hurt, but my assailant would have suffered more if I had not got between him and the householder, who was set to give him a real hiding!

Summer holidays in much of the southern hemisphere start just after Christmas so December is often a climax for church activity before the summer camps. In Mapucheland congregations often met together for a 'concentration' when new Christians would be baptized and received into membership, in the knowledge that it might be a year or two before the bishop came for confirmation.

I led the 1957 concentration, which took place in the church run by Segundo Nahuelpi in Repucura. He was a saintly man and a very effective evangelist who stayed with us one winter's night in Cholchol. As we listened to him by our fireside, Marj and I were moved by his outstanding faith that carried him through much adversity. He told us of the loss of most of his animals. But he said, quoting the prophet Habakkuk, 'though there are no sheep in the pen and no cattle in the stalls, yet I will rejoice in the Lord, I will be joyful in God my Saviour.' We could be forgiven for feeling that an Old Testament prophet had come among us. To quote Barbara Bazley's description of Segundo: 'He walked enormous distances wearing homemade sandals whose soles were made of car tyres. Yet he was a prophet and a visionary. He had planted churches and led many other Mapuches to faith in Christ.' Segundo worked at a correspondence course on the Bible but often got his answers wrong, and he wrote at the bottom of one paper, 'I'm afraid I'm not very good at lessons, but last week I conducted an evangelistic campaign and 16 souls were led to God, Alleluia.'[10]

We had a lovely service outside his wooden church on the hillside and then went to the stream for the baptisms. A number of people were received into church member-ship, which meant, among other things, that they would then be able to receive holy communion when a clergyman was available. The irony was that I, as a lay missionary, could receive them, but that apart from two elderly Mapuche priests, none of the other local pastors had been ordained to celebrate the sacraments. I felt then and still do, that godly people like Segundo, who proved themselves as evangelists and pastors, should have been ordained to the ministry of the word and sacrament.

There was a shift towards this after our time, through the vision of Tony Barratt with his team. Bishop Daniel Ivor Evans also mellowed to the idea. He had once argued with me that a priest is ordained into the whole Church of God and can therefore minister in the whole Church; he would not therefore ordain an Indian unless he could minister in a place like Oxford. I came to the conclusion that, ordination belongs to the universal Church, but the appointment or licensing is to the appropriate local congregation. So there was no need to prepare everyone for Oxford! I had no doubt that Segundo had the potential to be an effective priest, as well as a pastor, in Repucura, where he was already fulfilling a lay ministry. Three years later Canon Harry Sutton told me that he had elicited a more positive response from Bishop Evans, who said, 'Show me a man who can lift his brethren and I will ordain him.' Perhaps the bishop hoped that through God's grace I might be able to do that when he said that he would ordain me on my return to South America.

Notes

1 This has to do with a portrait of Christ, which remained intact during a bad earthquake and it was believed to have miraculous powers for protection against the dreaded earthquakes.

2 The temptation is always to feel that people need missionaries if they are different from us. The fact is that we all need the Gospel because we are all so much alike as part of fallen humanity.

3 I last visited her in 1951, when following a stroke she could only express herself through her eyes, the recitation of a few hymns, the

Lord's Prayer and her phrase of greeting: 'Well, well, well!'

4 Bird manure.

5 Deuteronomy 19.14.

6 I understand that he also had a special saddle desk made to enable writing on journeys!

7 See Chapter 1, page 15.

8 Tony Barratt wrote in the SAMS Annual Report: 'As we think back over the mighty blessings and victories that God has vouchsafed to us at Cholchol and all in the compass of a year, it just seems like a wonderful dream. Month after month the evangelists have returned with joyful hearts to tell of the latest victories granted by the Lord. How we praised His Name as we saw the little Churches being born in Coyimco, Chacamo, Coigue, Rupucura, Chivilcoyan, Conoco, Tranahuillin and Fundo Canada. Reports also came back of even greater blessings granted to the existing Churches at Malalche, also Cautinche to a lesser degree. Finally the evangelists returned from Pelal, not far from Quepe and Ilhui where The Lord has continued to manifest His saving power.'

9 An English translation of the proceedings of that conference, The Apostolic Work, was published by SAMS in 1958.

10 Barbara Bazley, Hidden Gold, Pickering & Inglis 1985, p. 56.

4
ENGLAND

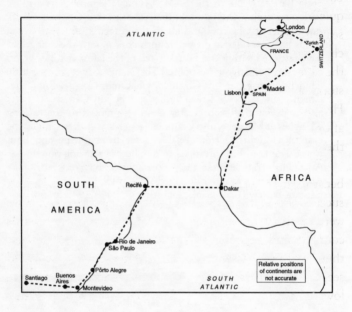

Heading home

Our Santiago to London flight, described by KLM as only 20 hours' flying time, actually took from a 5 a.m. departure on the Saturday to late afternoon arrival on Monday. Just in time for Christmas 1957. We crossed the Andes to Buenos Aires and then put down at all the major cities up the east coast before heading east early Sunday morning towards Dakar in West Africa. By way of variety our seating was occasionally rearranged without warning while we were on the ground. It was almost like a party game as we looked to see where the overhead luggage had been put! For a while we were alongside an Italian who disturbed everybody by shouting at his wife for not keeping their baby quiet, then beside an elderly lady who told me how quick this flight was compared to her first journey by seaplane to Brazil just after the war. I later sat beside a fascinating Jewish man who was one of the few survivors of the Warsaw rising in Poland when Stalin deliberately stopped his armies to abandon them to the Nazi massacre. He had become a prosperous businessman who could afford £30 for one of the beds which were available in those vintage planes.

There was subdued panic in Dakar on the Sunday because four planes had unexpectedly arrived in quick succession and the airport had run out of food. When we were eventually taxiing for take off at 4 p.m., the stewards counted and recounted us with worried looks because there was one passenger missing. After a while we could see a little jeep racing up the runway and the steps were lowered for our Jewish friend to climb in. He sheepishly explained, amid his fluster, that he had just gone for a quiet picnic! Perhaps it was his unpredictability that had enabled him to escape the Holocaust. Further stops in Spain and Portugal got us to Zurich at 2 a.m. on Monday morning, too late for our London connection, so we were taken to a hotel to rest before the afternoon plane.

Mission on the periphery

It took me a while to get back into English ways. Punctuality was never my strong point, so it suited me that nothing happened on time in Chile where we did not say that we missed the bus, but that the bus or train left us. 'El tren me dejo' sounds much kinder! The growing materialism surprised me. People were still wearing their utility suits from the war years and there had been few luxuries when I had left England in 1951.

My biggest shock was the impact of television, which I had not seen before. We had been looking forward to long fireside chats to catch up on family news and share something of our life with our parents. But the little box with its black and white picture had usurped the focus of the fireside and bedtime came around with very little conversation. Nor did I, at that time, find it easy to read or study while the TV was on.

It was lovely to be back with our family and to meet so many old friends in the village, but when I went to church on Sunday I felt frustrated by the seeming complacency of the service. Church life had changed very little and for me the swansong of the Church of England seemed to be, 'As it was in the beginning, is now and ever shall be, world without end, Amen.' The Church Assembly (which would give way to a General Synod of the Church of England) had spent a lot of its time on Archbishop Fisher's concern to revise our ancient canon law. Debates on what clergymen should wear in church generated more heat than light and to get the canons passed it was stated that vestments like the coloured stole had no doctrinal significance! I noticed that while evangelicals were still the naughty boys of the Church of England, they were making a significant impact on church life. Dr Billy Graham's first major mission[1] in the UK had produced a generation of young evangelical Christians. The Revd Dr John Stott, rector of All Souls',

Langham Place, was leading many clergy from a defensive, backs-to-the-wall attitude to a positive commitment within the church.

Things were happening in SAMS. The society was considered to be very peripheral by most bishops. Its own president had suggested that the operation be wound up. Clifford Martin, the evangelical bishop of Liverpool, cautioned a clergyman, 'You don't want to give your life to a dying cause.'[2] Even John Weller, the previous Anglican bishop in South America, wrote pessimistically: '. . . SAMS has mission stations among the Indians in the far north of the Argentine and in Paraguay. The Indians in these parts are of a much lower standard of humanity than the Mapuche. They are nomadic tribes with a variety of languages but gradually civilization is creeping upon them and in the long run they will be absorbed into the Argentine and Paraguayan nations. I see no future for any Anglican Church in these areas.'[3]

We saw things differently, and I was not at all put out by a letter from SAMS saying that while we should have a month's holiday before my preaching engagements, they would be very grateful if before then I could attend and speak at the SAMS annual conference. Goodwin Hudson set a relaxed tone as he sauntered into the opening meeting of the conference, sat at the piano and asked, 'Anybody got a hymn?' One of the young people present was Horace 'Race' Busk, whose uncle, a rancher in Paraguay, had given land to the SAMS mission there. Race was inspired by the conference and he subsequently enthused his fellow theological students like Pat Harris, Maurice Jones and Michael Vernon, who became key missionaries in South America.

A sympathetic priest

As we would be living with Marj's parents in Blackpool for most of our home leave, Goody Hudson's wife, Dr Eleanor, told me to contact the vicar at St Mark's Church, Blackpool. He had a curate called Jack Wardle who could speak Spanish and I should persuade him to return to South America! The Lord had other plans. Jack became an influential supporter of SAMS and it was the vicar, Harry Sutton, who would ere long become general secretary of the society.

I was studying for ordination through Wolsey Hall, Oxford but I was also concerned about my lack of pastoral training. It later transpired that I would be working 500 miles away from the nearest clergyman and 1,000 miles from the bishop who would be responsible for directing me as a young deacon in charge of a chaplaincy church in Paraguay. The bishop suggested that I could get all the practical experience I needed if as a layman I spent some time with a sympathetic priest!

Who better than Harry Sutton? In 18 months his church had become one of the best attended in Blackpool. In the limited time I had with Harry he taught me things I never forgot, like 'Never be late at a funeral – it might be your umpteenth funeral but it's somebody's only mother.' We talked about the particular need at that time for a metropolitan secretary for SAMS and I was thrilled when Harry and his wife Olive, who had prayed about this, felt that God was leading him to volunteer.

Our return to South America was delayed, first because a streptococci infection put me in hospital for two weeks, and then Marj, who was expecting Andrew, our second child, was told by the doctor that she ought not to travel in view of her previous miscarriage. So SAMS asked me if I could spend six months making the society known in the north-west. Peter Tonge, a young clergyman in Liverpool who gave me invaluable advice and encouragement, suggested that I organize a north-west SAMS rally. Linked to that we invited 20 clergy for an afternoon tea at Reece's Café to meet Goodwin Hudson. Harry Sutton brought a busload from Blackpool for the rally and gave the final address. We knew that of likely speakers for SAMS he would draw most people.

Preparing for Paraguay

Meanwhile, Tony Barratt suggested that besides overseeing the farm in Chile I should organize a Bible school for the training of leaders. I looked forward to the opportunity to learn more while teaching in the Bible school. But Goody was more concerned about the work in Paraguay, where our treasurer and others had pressed for a complete withdrawal by SAMS. He presented us with a completely new challenge. Would Marj and I go to the capital, Asuncion, where two new missionaries, Dorothea Wedgwood and Jocelyn Padbury, had discovered that the chaplaincy church was in the trust of SAMS?

Our departure was almost delayed because Andrew, like all our babies, was late, but the doctor was insistent that we should not cancel our sailing: 'The sooner you are on your way, the better for the baby to acclimatize to the new surroundings.' Everything came together at the end. Andrew was born on 19 February. I returned home from the Liverpool rally two days later to find that Marj had

discharged herself from hospital, so as to give me instruc-
tions on the packing. She also attended her sister Pat's
wedding on 28 February, before we left Blackpool late that
evening with our old car packed full, en route for
Southampton docks, via Somerset. Unfortunately, like our
previous car, it expired at a most inconvenient moment.
The breakdown man, whose wife was a Sunday school
teacher, said we could spend the rest of that night in their
home. He would sell the car for scrap. Next morning I
packed and despatched our luggage by road haulier to my
parents' home. Then we got the train to London for our
valedictory service and travelled back late that night by
the last train to Salisbury, where my brother collected us.
We had two days in Somerset, sorting out final things
and saying fond farewells, then my brother and father
drove us to board the luxurious *Andes* in Southampton.
All that with a baby less than two weeks old! I should have
been more cautious in my planning and, with hindsight,
more demanding upon SAMS for the proper provision
of transport. But I had been reared in a culture of 'make
do and mend'.

Notes

1 He had conducted missions in the UK with Youth For Christ in the
    late 1940s.
2 That clergyman did not join the staff but he became an outstanding
    life-long supporter of the society.
3 The Southwell diocesan journal, October 1946.

5
PARAGUAY

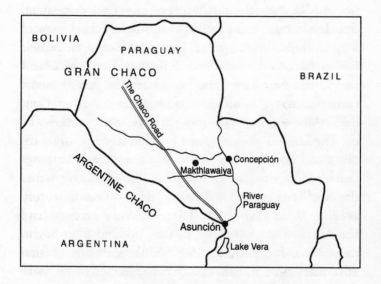

A threefold challenge

Life in Paraguay was very different from Chile. Our first house had two large rooms, a rustic kitchen and a bathroom. Marj cheerfully tackled her multiple chores as she made the house into a home. Cooking on a primus stove was not easy. Some of the vegetable shopping was from a lady who brought goods on a donkey, but most came from the 5 a.m. visits to the market. Little Richenda seemed to enjoy herself and baby Andrew thrived.

Bureaucracy was a bugbear. A small postal package took 26 distinct operations in several departments before it was cleared. One needed certificates to show that we had complied with different laws and contributions, including the payment of a tax in lieu of 14 days' citizen's service in road building, etc. But apart from that we liked Paraguay.

Goodwin Hudson had indicated a threefold challenge for us. We would initially serve the English-speaking church, although our main brief was the establishment of a Spanish-speaking ministry. He also expected me to give full support to the mission among the Lengua people in the Chaco where Derek and Betty Hawksbee maintained a faithful ministry in difficult circumstances. But for them, the SAMS work in Paraguay might have been closed down.

The English work required tact and tenacity. My mention that I hoped to start services in the Spanish language caused consternation. Unlike many Free Church people, the Anglicans in South America did not usually see any need to share their faith. They were very supportive of the Anglican mission work to the Amerindian tribes in the Chaco, but they certainly didn't want any of 'that missionary stuff' in their church. They seemed oblivious to the number of unchurched people, let alone immigrants. However, a nearby Protestant family from Czechoslovakia encouraged me to start services in Spanish. I would later face similar misgivings in Peru where one old-timer who seldom went to church said, 'What you don't understand, bishop, is that the Peruvians have got into the Phoenix [gentlemen's] Club, they are in the cricket club, and now you want to bring them into the church!' St Andrew's, the chaplaincy church in Paraguay, was known locally as 'the church that never opens its doors'.

In the midst of all these early difficulties, a Bible verse jumped out at me from St Paul's second letter to Timothy:

'The servant of the Lord must not strive; but be gentle unto all men, apt to teach, patient, in meekness instructing those that oppose themselves.'[1]

The British people living in and around Asuncion included the commercial and diplomatic contingent, who seemed to spend most evenings at cocktail parties. The long-term settlers did not normally attend those functions. Some of them struggled to make ends meet. When the Duke of Edinburgh visited Paraguay, the ambassador was naturally anxious to include all the British folk at a reception. It seems that I was the only person who could introduce him to most of the long-term residents. Some were real characters. Everyone knew the Insleys. Ninety-year-old Tom had waited, rather impatiently, with his sisters Emmy and Julie for Prince Philip to get round to their corner of the embassy grounds. When he asked them, 'How long have you been here?' Julie responded, 'A whole half an hour, waiting for you.' With a chuckle the Prince said, 'No, no, I meant when did you arrive in Paraguay?' The sisters then differed on whether it was at the turn of the previous century or the early 1890s.

My first ministry to the Paraguayans was in an area called Mariano Roque Alonso, about 15 miles from our home. It had no church of any sort and I set aside one day a week for house-to-house visiting there. A matriarchal lady, Dona Rosa, agreed to invite neighbours for Sunday afternoon classes on her patio. Her husband, Alfonso, was away for weeks on end as a long distance cattle drover. He was the sort of hard-living cowboy one expected to see in Wild West films.

All sorts of things can happen in a new mission. The bishop had given me a dozen prayer books published in

Spanish by the SPCK and there was just under a dozen people in the congregation when I started services in Asuncion. I was half-way through the sermon when one lady decided to gather up all the books and take them with her. No one else quite knew what to do, so with an apology I broke off the sermon, chased down the street after her, recouped the precious books and then returned to my place at the front of the congregation. No one else seemed to think that there was anything unusual about all that! God seemed to send us a high percentage of wounded creatures and unusual characters. But then, a missionary should not quarrel with his raw material.

New life and growth

Everything happened at once in July 1961. I was working with a professional photographer for a SAMS film. Our third baby, Rachel, like the rest of our children, arrived late, a whole month overdue. She had obligingly waited until the filming was finished, by which time Marj had persuaded the local doctor that castor oil could be a useful means of starting the birth process, as it had been with Andrew. It worked, and I was present at Rachel's birth at around 3 a.m. next morning. I regret that I had not been present for the birth of our other children, and also that at Rachel's I spent my time at the end of the room, worrying whether the doctor was doing his work properly, instead of holding Marj's hand.

Marj came out of hospital two days later, as Harry Sutton arrived for his first visit to us. Our colleague Derek Hawksbee brought a crocodile's tail from the Chaco and cooked a delicious meal. It tasted like something between pork and fish and not everyone knew what they were eating!

Harry's visit marked a turning point for SAMS and between 1961 and 1963 we received 12 new missionaries, more than the total sent to Paraguay in the previous 20 years. Fred and Jessica Train, who had served in the Chaco, also returned to Asuncion. Fred had a key role in preparing Indians to be ordained for ministry to their own people.

Fred and I decided to drive up the new Chaco road, across to Makthlawaiya following bullock cart tracks and then over to Concepcion. It was such a relief to travel with someone who knew the hazards of the Chaco, like watching out for palm stumps in the long grass. We arrived at Makthlawaiya without mishap and later drove eastward to Concepcion. We had been told that there would be no difficulty crossing the River Paraguay, but it was a hair-raising experience. Two rowing boats pulled up parallel to each other near the bank. Planks were put across these at right angles, and I had to drive down on to them. Two men then sat at the back of the boats and rowed us across. We were in front!

Jocelyn Padbury and Glenys Williams had moved to Concepcion, the main river port for most of the Chaco. They had started a small school and established an Anglican church in what was then Paraguay's second city. My earlier exploratory visit to Concepcion had been poignant because one of my best friends from All Nations, Brian Stokes, had died there very suddenly from a viral infection that seemed like a bad attack of flu. He left a widow and young family. His mission was the only protestant church in the city and I stayed with his successor, who greatly encouraged us with our plans.

Concepcion had depended upon a weekly river steamer for travel to Asuncion until the Paraguayan army initiated a passenger service with DC3s, the longest serving twin engine planes around at that time. The one on the Concepcion run was equipped for parachutists and the passengers sat in the bucket seats along the sides. There was a rail overhead to which the soldiers' parachutes would be fixed ready for release as they went out of the rear door. The motto over the door into the pilot's cabin, 'vencer or morir' (win or die), didn't really seem appropriate for civilian passengers!

Thea Wedgwood started a small English-speaking kindergarten in what had been my office in St Andrew's, Asuncion. Year on year this developed into the Colegio San Andres, with full primary and secondary levels. The college enjoys a good reputation, thanks to a dedicated Christian staff with bilingual teaching. Pupils have included grandchildren of presidents, ministers of education and other influential Paraguayans. I was proud to have a part in the enterprise but it did not seem right to me that we should subsidize an élite school with mission funds. I argued that the school would gain in prestige if, in view of its outstanding quality, it also charged the highest fees in the country. This would enable deserving pupils from poorer homes to receive bursaries. The school also set an example to other prestige schools by establishing an annexe for free education in one of the poorest parts of Asuncion.

Thanks to the support of Tony Barratt, Alberto Mena, a young Mapuche evangelist, joined us for a year. He was a most effective worker. On Fridays I would go out with him to talk to people who had shown interest during the week and several small church groups came into being. Not all continued, but it is thrilling to see lively churches today where we started those small meetings.

Tragedy and change

After five years we were due for home leave. We were aware that changes were afoot in the Anglican Church, partly due to the demise of Daniel Ivor Evans. He had died in a tragic accident. His overnight bus from Temuco to Santiago in Chile stopped because he was feeling unwell. No one realized that it had stopped on a bridge without any sidewalks or balustrades. The bishop just disappeared over the edge. He was still alive when they retrieved him from the boulders below but he sadly expired before reaching the next town.

Later in 1963, a conference, chaired by the then Archbishop of York, Donald Coggan, proposed sweeping changes for the future of Anglican work, including the formation of new dioceses. I knew that this would affect Paraguay and felt that while I had been involved in the growth of our work someone with more maturity should carry it forward. SAMS agreed to my suggestion that Canon Tony Barratt (as he then was) might succeed me as mission superintendent. Tony accepted and we left Paraguay on 23 December 1963, grateful indeed for all that God was doing and would do through the Chaco mission and the nascent Anglican Church in urban areas.

Note

1   2 Timothy 2.24, AV.

6
ARGENTINA

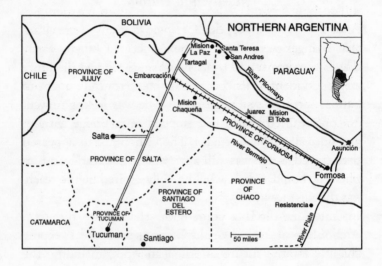

Uncertainties

We arrived back in England from Paraguay in January 1964 to meet with Harry Sutton, Doug Milmine, Tony Barratt and Major Batt, then chairman of SAMS. The main item on our agenda was the likely changes in South America. Kenneth Howell had been appointed bishop of Chile, Peru and Bolivia, and Cyril Tucker bishop of Eastern South America with the Falkland Islands. This was the first step towards more manageable missionary episcopates.

The uncertainty about our future was settled by a

request from missionaries in northern Argentina. Francis Tompkins, their superintendent, was going to remain in England because of health problems and they asked if we could join them. We accepted, but another worrying health problem loomed large. Marj was slowing down while I was still rushing around. When I said, 'I want to burn out for God,' she tellingly replied, 'I know, but you are scorching me in the process.' She was expecting the birth of our fourth baby and found the pregnancy particularly demanding. Her doctor prescribed a blood transfusion for anaemia but showed little sympathy when she told him that she was finding difficulty even in cleaning her teeth. After she produced another beautiful daughter, Rosalind Helen, we both had another medical check with a different doctor, who declared us fit. I asked him if he really felt that Marj was all right and he replied, 'Yes, but you must watch her anaemia.' I resolved to watch it, but how?

We had to return to Paraguay to sort out our belongings and arrange the move, and I made a preparatory visit to northern Argentina. Within two weeks of our arrival in Asuncion, Tony and his wife Peggy talked to me about Marj, who they had not seen for six years. Her weight, puffy eyes and lethargy concerned Tony. It turned out that he had spotted these same symptoms, which indicated thyroid deficiency, in Peggy several years before! The doctor at the Baptist hospital concurred with his diagnosis but said that first of all he wanted to make sure she was not suffering from pernicious anaemia. Thankfully she wasn't and we were blessed that a daily tablet would maintain the thyroid balance. He believed that Marj could soon have gone into an irreversible coma. Years later she spotted the same early symptoms in our Richenda and insisted that she went to her doctor. He was a little scathing when he asked her why she had come and she said, 'because my mother told me to'. He did prescribe a blood test and told her to come back in three months' time, but within the week she was called back and put on thyroxin immediately. As so often happens, 'Mother was right!' We still trust our English doctors and feel passionately committed to the NHS. Perhaps their oversight in our case was due to the fact that they practise in a situation where the opposite problem of over-active thyroid seems to be more common.

Marj stayed on in Asuncion while the hospital did periodic checks. Where others might have grumbled at living out of a suitcase, she commented on how we could get by without all the accoutrements which we love to have around us.

Mision Chaquena

Meanwhile I got to know most of our new area. I had visited the centre of our mission in Algarrobal, also known as Mision Chaquena, in 1960. It had been a long haul in those days. The weekly riverboat took me to the flat and humid provincial capital of Formosa to get the train across the Chaco. It was an experience to travel on one of the oldest railways in South America. Twice a week the wood-fuelled steam engine went up and down the 500 miles of straight narrow gauge track.[1] The train was seldom punctual; the 8 a.m. departure from Formosa depended on whether it was ready in time and the intended arrival next day at 6 a.m. was subject, among other things, to whether we hit any cows on the journey. Animals were reasonably safe when they slept on the line. The driver could see them and frighten them off with long whistle blasts, which woke us in our bunks, as the brakes were applied. But disaster often loomed for cattle asleep and unseen in the tall grass or scrub alongside the route. They would be startled and confused by the train's lights at the last moment. The protective grill or cowcatcher at the front of the engine seldom seemed to prevent their entanglement and occasionally the train would be derailed.

The train stopped at 28 small towns that had grown up between Embarcacion and Formosa. There were growing Wichi and Toba Indian settlements around most of these places. A mission station was established at one of these, called Ingeniero Juarez. An earth road was later built alongside the railway and there was a Wild West feel about the area. To quote from a later letter home in April 1967: 'Whenever I go down the line there always seems to be a batch of recent scandals including one or two murders. Life is awful and cheap. This time, however, it was comical to find that the chief of police (in Juarez) was detained in his own prison. He had knocked a cow down on the road and then he and his companions decided that the best thing to do was to make the best of a bad job! David Leake, who had been called in to witness the formal confession, came back chuckling about the phrase in the declaration that "He" (the chief of police) "then proceeded to have a succulent barbecue". The civil registrar in another town was also in jail for falsifying papers!'

The fresh, pre-dawn sub-tropical air invigorated me as I arrived on that first visit to Mision Chaquena. The six-mile drive through the scrub from the Padre Lozano station was on a narrow track which was being upgraded to an elevated earth road. The missionaries had strung out a welcome

sheet over the entrance to the large mission house, which
read 'Welcome', with its Wichi equivalent 'Amtena'. Not
many people get that treatment at six o'clock in the
morning. Little did I realize that five years later, Marj and
I would spend some of our happiest days there.

'Conference' was a grand word for a meeting of eight
missionaries, whose number was soon to be halved as
both couples of the small team were to leave shortly. The
Revd John and Ester Bradbury were concerned about the
education of their two boys. Before he left, John wrote to
SAMS proposing a new mission policy, which by building
on what had gone before could transform the work. He
urged that there should be a firm commitment to the
ordination of Wichi pastors and that missionaries should no
longer be placed in lonely outstations to serve as general
factotum of schoolteacher, medical attendant, pastor (lay
or ordained) and administrator. Harry Sutton picked this
up and he encouraged Francis Tompkins, the new superintendent, to plan to place new missionaries in three key
centres for regular visits to the Indian villages, which were
spread over a vast area. Their individual skills and training
would be applied to support the churches and train people
for service in medicine, basic education and ministry.

Consequently, there was a completely new spirit when
I returned to give more Bible readings in 1962. A dynamic
team surrounded Francis, a gentle man, who had grown
up among the Wichi.

Now I was back in Mision Chaquena for a briefing by
Canon Alfred Leake. He and his wife Dorothy had spent
most of their working lives together in the Chaco. Their
return towards the end of their ministry, after a spell in

England, came at a time when we had a lot to learn from them. He had purchased land on the outskirts of Embarcacion where we later erected three prefabricated buildings which could be enlarged with the help of Indian craftsmen. Meanwhile we would live in the old mission station 25 miles away.

I visited Canon Leake's son David and his wife Rachel who were in charge at Juarez, further down the line. They invariably provided most relaxing and gracious hospitality and I greatly enjoyed my stay with them and their children. We attended a service at the Mataco Indian settlement on the southern outskirts of the town and visited a Toba settlement on the north side. Juarez is laid out in the traditional style, with about 35 blocks divided by wide earth roads. The small hospital served the Indians as well as the white settlers, to the best of its ability. The school had its square and the police station took up half a block. It had a cage-like lock-up, that helped in hot weather, but this was visible from the street, so that anyone could see who happened to be inside.

A constant flow of Indian folk started arriving around 7 a.m. and sat in front of the Leakes' home. They would wait, knitting or weaving, and talking among themselves, while Rachel chatted to each in turn about their concerns. A number would have relatives needing medical help, others just wanted to unload some burden or even a memory from the past, which, as was their custom, they would tell as if it had just happened. It was not always apparent whether immediate action was required or whether they were just unburdening themselves. The unexpected and the unscheduled were the norm for David and Rachel as they gave themselves so completely to the people. One day it was suppertime before they realized that they had forgotten to stop for lunch!

The question of ordination

My next journey kept me on the move for two months. During the first stage Pat Harris introduced Tony Barratt and me to his area as the three of us visited the string of Indian villages alongside the Pilcomayo River. The Indian church leaders impressed me as we travelled from village to village. Alberto, a clever and godly man at Mision San Andres, seemed to have learnt so much with so few books. Henry Grubb, who had spotted Alberto's ability in the 1950s, wrote, 'Alberto had already proved himself to be a scholar, but his method of correcting my attempts to translate the Mataco New Testament set the seal upon his remarkable ability.'[2] Alberto seemed younger than the other leaders but sadly he died of heart failure as he was walking into Mision Chaquena to become director of the Bible school.

Mariano, another lovely leader, had moved in his early twenties from Mision San Andres to a non-Christian group who wanted to know about the faith. Through his teaching the village of Santa Teresa became Christian and a church was built with rooms for visitors alongside. Those who stayed in those rooms sometimes heard Mariano praying very early in the morning, as he mentioned all the members of the village by name. On a later visit I was taking my time sorting out a few things for the journey. Mariano came to my room and said, 'Guillermo, we must have prayers soon because the people need to go into the forest to find food or they will be hungry at the end of the day.'

I mused wrongly that although they lived at such a subsistence level their village and the church was safe above the high riverbanks. But these had built up from silt, which sloped away from the riverbed, and in the mid-1980s the river suddenly changed course further upstream. It swept through the village without warning. Dear old Mariano just wanted to stay in his church but the younger men waded in and carried him physically to higher ground. He was old and failing in sight when I visited their new settlement in 1988 but he recognized my voice and he threw his arms around me. We just hugged and tried to keep back the tears. He always treated me like a son.

Further upstream at La Paz, the pastoral sensitivity of David Gonzalez, a Wichi married to a Chunupi, enabled him to minister to three previously warring tribal groups. He had the ability to represent their feelings to the wider world. Carlos and Ernesto, two older men, also ministered to their community of Santa Maria. A long white loincloth enhanced Ernesto's quiet dignity at his ordination. He probably never wore western trousers in his life. A Jesuit priest who visited Santa Maria when Ernesto celebrated holy communion told David Leake that he had received the bread and wine. As he put it, 'How could I not partake as I observed the godliness of the man who consecrated the bread so reverently with his worn hands?'[3]

The question of ordination had dominated our conversation on the trip. Pat was troubled by the expectation that he should follow the pattern of the previous ordained missionaries, who travelled by horseback to celebrate very infrequent communion services in Indian villages. It looked

as if celebrating communion was something which only
white missionaries could do. Roland Allan's books had
influenced me. He had been a SPG (Society for the
Propagation of the Gospel) missionary in China and subsequently spent most of his life trying to persuade the
church that the New Testament practice of ordaining
leaders where churches had recently been formed could be
applicable in our time. Canon Leake had previously talked
with me about the need to ordain Indian leaders but felt
that the shared oversight, along the Plymouth Brethren
pattern, would be more appropriate because he rightly
pointed out that to raise one individual above their colleagues could cause problems in the Indian culture. He
became positively excited when I said that I could see no
reason why, where appropriate, two or three Indians could
not be ordained for a shared ministry. That was indeed to
happen in some villages.

There was another cultural consideration. The Bible
school in Mision Chaquena was training younger men
who had been selected under the guidance of the older
leaders. Should they now be ordained to take over from
those Fathers in God who had sent them? And would the
people accept their authority? Our new bishop, Cyril
Tucker, said with some logic that our church could not
have it both ways. It could not claim to be a eucharistic
church and then refuse to ordain local leaders to minister
the sacraments. He readily agreed that he would ordain the
established leaders first. The younger men in training
would be ordained as deacons and sent back to support
them in church.

I had once listened to a Radio Four interview with
Donald Marsh, the Bishop of the Arctic, who made annual

trips to recruit clergy from England. He said that he was unable to ordain Eskimos (Inuit) as clergy because they could not speak English! I felt that there was something wrong in his thinking. So years later I was very moved when the Anglican Church of Canada observed what we were doing in the selection, ordination and ongoing training of Indian clergy and invited me to visit their outstanding bishop, Doug Hambidge, to encourage him in his plans for the ordination of Canadian Indians.[4]

I had to go to Chile for a conference before arriving back in Paraguay to find that Marj was in bed with hepatitis, as was Richenda. She had probably contracted the infection at school. The big shock as I walked into our bedroom was not the yellow of Marj's complexion but the fact that thanks to the effective treatment for her thyroid problems, plus a strict diet, she had dropped from 14 to 7 stones. I soon realized that all her old energy was restored in spite of hepatitis. Bedrest while others looked after the children was essential, but not easy during the recuperation period.

Developments

We eventually arrived as a family in Mision Chaquena. We enjoyed the simple lifestyle and one Sunday evening as Marj and I walked across the patio after church she said, 'I could live here forever'. I remember the moment because we then went indoors and started to put things up on the living room wall. Marj bent down to pick up an artificial flower and almost touched a snake. With a petrified 'Look out!' she pointed to its sinister colour and the stripes that went all around its belly, indicating that it was a true and deadly coral. I confess to no compunction about killing poisonous snakes, especially with the awful contemplation of what might have happened when Marj was so close to touching it, or had little Rossy been crawling on the floor. We gradually realized that our children were, by law of averages, far safer in the mission than elsewhere. They soon learnt basic survival rules, such as, 'Never go across the yard to the outside loo without a good torch when it is dark'. 'Always shake out anything from your shoes before putting them on' (in case of spiders or scorpions), and 'always use a mosquito net'. Even on mosquito-free nights there were still the vinchucas (a sort of flying bedbug which hides in dark crevices). They don't leave a mark, but if you walked around next day with an awful head it was more than likely that you had provided a feast of blood during the night.

When we moved to Embarcacion we stupidly became less vigilant about snakes and sadly Valerie Pilbrow (now Mrs Val Harris) paid a frightful price when she stepped out of our prefab to walk the three yards to her room. She let out a yell and said that a toad had hurt her, but Marj pointed out the snake curled up in a corner as I saw the tooth marks across her ankle. It was a large yarara, which had the ability to open its jaws wide across a person's foot. The following 48 hours were horrific. We took Val in the back of the jeep to the local hospital and the ever helpful Dr Cutardi did his utmost in treatment. He was fearful that gangrene would set in because the poison was concentrated in one area, but thankfully we were able to bring Val home after a few days, leg intact but badly bruised.

In 1925 a certain William Everitt sold his builder's business in Norfolk, gave the proceeds to SAMS and went to serve as one of their missionaries for 31 years in the Argentine Chaco. He was no linguist but he could turn his hand to anything; for instance, straightening out a damaged front axle of a car, which another missionary had wrapped around a tree trunk. He got a fire going alongside the track in the middle of the Chaco and heated the axle enough to hammer it back into shape. He taught the Indians carpentry, and there are many rustic benches similar to his still in use by the Indians. It was his lathe, inherited by a quiet Indian called Delfin, that inspired our first visitor from Oxfam to grant enough money for me to set up a collection of power-driven tools. These included a bandsaw, plane and lathes, driven by a Perkins three-cylinder electric generator which I purchased 1,000 miles away in Buenos Aires. The project became known as Guillermo's co-operative. I liked that, because William Everitt and I shared the Spanish equivalent of William. I returned to Algarrobal during the winter holidays to install the equipment. We worked out a system whereby the Indians paid for every 15 minutes of usage. There would be a queue of craftsmen with logs, which they had brought up from the river on their wooden handcarts, for cutting to the right size to make chairs according to the pattern initiated by William Everitt.

Before the mechanization of the sugar estates the Indian tribal people from northern Argentina and Bolivia would migrate to the cane fields during the cutting season. An old Indian told me that the whole village, including women and children, would walk southwards through the forest for two or three weeks, hunting small prey and eating what might be available by way of scrubs. Where a foreigner would quickly lose his way and perish, they knew how to survive in the drought-ridden forest. Lagoons are few and far between but the Wichi can spot the thin, shrivelled stalk of a tuber, which is high in moisture content. 'But', continued the old man after a pause, 'those days are gone.' Survival in the villages has become much harder. Ecological damage has reduced the fish that come up the river to spawn and parts of the Chaco territory are being exploited by multinational combines. It is all highly mechanized with no need for Indian labour.

SAMS supported a dynamic, well-educated, evangelical missionary team of medics, educationalists, clergy and good all-rounders whose spiritual conviction strengthened their social commitment. They aimed at encouraging and enabling the Indian leadership to serve and represent their communities as part of Argentina.

Barbara Kitchen had concentrated upon setting up basic schools along the Pilcomayo by appointing some of the literate adults as teachers. She produced primers in the Indians' own language and I saw the thrill of young teenagers when these were put into their hands as the first book they had ever handled. Argentine Christians joined our team through Barbara's inspiration. Sylvia Roitberg, the first of these, was still studying for her doctorate in education when she got a job in the national school at Juarez, which was a good base to support Barbara's educational vision. Sylvia earned more as a government employee, but she sought to live on the same financial basis as the rest of the team. It was a sort of open religious community. We lived our independent lives while enjoying the best of communal trust and fellowship.

Dr Michael Patterson and the nurses increasingly

involved the Argentine ministry of health in medical development, so that when missionaries left, the government often put in national replacements, including a doctor at La Paz and auxiliary Indian nurses in Mision Chaquena and Juarez. Training Indian paramedics for isolated villages was initially little more than how to use a thermometer, administer aspirin and when and how to give injections. The system worked so well that some auxiliaries were accepted for further training and financed by the government. But to make this possible the candidates needed basic primary education in the Spanish language. The little schooling they might have had was constantly interrupted through the nomadic pressure of casual labour. We suspended the Bible school for two years so that promising young Wichi could come in with their families and the husbands (who were seen as the breadwinners) would cover primary education to the government's satisfaction in a two-year course. Some were then accepted for further training and became recognized medical auxiliaries. Meanwhile Barbara persuaded the federal authorities to produce informative radio programmes in the native language and she ensured that several Wichi women were given specific training for this.

It was not difficult to obtain grants for the purchase of vehicles for our medical team. The problem was how to find funding for running costs like basic medicines and petrol. Then, a marvellous mistake happened. Vernon Littlewood of Christian Aid flew all the way from London to a conference in Uruguay only to find that it had been cancelled. He had planned to look in on us anyway but now he had more time and, fortunately, I was at home when he arrived in Salta, the provincial capital, a week early. We visited most of the area and I explained my frustration of not being able to obtain basic funding to keep the work going. Vernon agreed to grants for ground clearing and irrigation and suggested that we should present a comprehensive plan for the entire social work.

The Revd Maurice Sinclair, who was trained in agriculture as well as theology, prepared a ten-year plan in consultation with the Indians and the missionary team. I presented this to the WCC (World Council of Churches) in Switzerland and aid agencies in Germany, as well as the English organizations, so that they could see where we were going. Christian Aid, to their credit, underwrote the vital but less exciting expenses of vehicle and administrative costs. The agricultural development proved difficult because we were so far away from the markets and the expense of sinking deep wells meant that Indian families could not go it alone. The simpler approach of intermediate technology was not generally applicable to agriculture in the Chaco but it was very relevant to carpentry. We learnt by our mistakes and my colleagues produced many positives, including educational developments which enabled a younger generation of Wichi to speak for themselves and their people. Alec Dean, one of the Argentine agriculturists, spotted the potential for the Indian craftwork and he now gives all his time to the development of this cottage industry.

Another move for the archdeacon

Marj and I needed to be at a focal point for the whole area and with school starting dates for our children in mind we moved into our home in Embarcacion before all the floors were finished, and without the provision of extra guest-rooms and an office. It was a strategic base because the passenger service on the Embarcacion to Formosa railway was still running and we were also on the road junction for the areas. We had a constant flow of missionary and Indian visitors, particularly when the train came in on Tuesdays and Fridays. Fortunately during that year Kevin Bewley, an Australian missionary, moved into Embarcacion for ministry to the Indian visitors. The nearby Indian settlers built a shelter on our site for their services in Mataco. Walter and Sally Robbins also joined us to establish a Spanish-speaking ministry for the townsfolk.

We felt settled and our children loved the very friendly state school, but within a year we were faced by an unexpected need in Salta. Michael and Elly Hobbs had moved there from Paraguay, where their eldest son was plagued by asthma. His condition was still troublesome and 12 months on they felt that they should return to England. We pondered on who should replace them and eventually thought about ourselves!

The move of the archdeacon, as I then was, to the provincial capital made sense, but we were hesitant to suggest it to the missionaries. We would be going from the tough, hot and dusty, Chaco conditions to a lovely small city nestled up in the eastern Andean foothills. As we prayed about it we felt that I, in my travels, should discuss this with each of the missionaries. They all felt that the move made sense. I still wondered about the Indians, who might feel that I was deserting them. It wasn't until 20 years later, when I went back on a visit, that my mind was settled on that score. Two of my Indian friends spontaneously reassured me. Colin Altamarino said, 'Guillermo, I remember when I was in difficulty with the military in Salta how you interceded for me.' I had completely forgotten the difficulties he had encountered. When the government gave Indians identity documents which recognized them as citizens some were automatically classified as criminals for not having done military service, which no one could do without identification documents! David Gonzalez, the wise old chief and pastor from La Paz, said, 'Guillermo, we were so grateful when you moved into Salta because then we had someone to represent us to the authorities. Before, there was no one.' That was not entirely true: Domingo Ferrari, a most helpful Methodist pastor, was always ready to speak on behalf of the Indians, and he gave me much needed support.

David Gonzalez was referring to something that had happened when we were under military rule. He and another Indian arrived in Salta just as I was about to set out on a Chaco trip. They were worried because an officer had arrived at Mision La Paz to tell them about his plans to concentrate all the Indians at Santa Maria, about 30 miles upstream where the government had plans for a major development project. He wanted them all to be ready for the transfer within two weeks. The intentions were good but the results would have been disastrous even if there had been a long-term implementation of the project. Indians need space for hunting in the forest and fishing in the river. Mision La Paz, their home village, was precious to them. Three Indian tribes, Wichi, Chunupi and Choroti, had learnt to live and worship together. What if they were all uprooted? With the help of Domingo I obtained an audience with the provincial governor that afternoon. I prayed hard! We were seated at a table and I spoke as tactfully and carefully as I could. The governor, who came over as a real gentleman, assured us that he had given no orders for the removal of the Indians and they could remain where they were. I asked him for a letter of assurance, which the Indians could take back to the Pilcomayo, to which he replied, 'You do not need a letter, my word is my bond.'

I did not doubt his integrity, but I was thrilled when the next day the local papers published a full report of our interview, along with his assurance that the Indians would not be moved. The two Indians took back copies to show their people but we still remained uneasy about the military plans for Santa Maria. These had not emanated from Salta but from federal offices in Buenos Aires a thousand miles away. So I visited the top echelon in Buenos Aires to offer whatever positive co-operation we could make. At first they were defensive, but gradually warmed as I outlined factors that could contribute to the success or failure of their plans. One of the officers confided that there was a natural suspicion of the English, bearing in mind that in the previous century we had ejected the Argentines from the Islas Malvinas (Falkland Islands). They felt we could well be making a pincer movement by our presence in the north. I could understand their feeling, even if that fear sounded incredible. I think that they accepted my assurance that nothing of the sort was in mind and that we were only there to serve. In fact, our hope was that a peaceful and just solution would be found over the Falkland Islands; even if in those pre-conflict days most English people thought that these islands were located somewhere near to the Orkneys.

Our youngest daughter Patty was born in Salta. The doctor assured us on 2 July 1968 that it would be several days before the birth and that I could fit in an urgent trip to the Chaco with no problems. I set out at 4.30 a.m. (just before Marj started labour pains!) and almost had an awful accident around 7 a.m. A stick of sugar cane fell from a lorry coming towards me, and I immediately anticipated that a boy waiting with his mother on my side of the road would run across to pick it up. I jammed on my brakes just in time and burst a tyre but the thought that I might have killed him was appalling. The telephone lines were down that day and I could not check on Marj, so when I eventually got home at 2.30 a.m. I was met at the door by Pat Harris who said 'Get to the clinic you have another little Billy!' Patty looked so much like me even at birth. But like all our girls, she got her beauty from Marj and my mother's side of the family!

Becoming a bishop

I sometimes travelled by bus and train to consult with Bishop Tucker in Buenos Aires, and his periodic visits to us for confirmations and ordinations were much appreciated. He and his wife Kathleen always made me think hard about my ideas and convictions but the vast distances left us very much to our own devices in the north. In 1969 he surprised me by asking if I would become bishop of a new diocese in Paraguay. He was disappointed when I didn't feel that I could accept this challenge. We were at a crucial stage in the development of the social work in northern Argentina and I was not at all sure that it would be right for me to go back to Paraguay where my good friend Tony

Barratt was exercising a visionary ministry. Meanwhile the bishop had asked David Leake to be his assistant as bishop in northern Argentina. After further discussions, I was asked if I would agree to being bishop in Paraguay and northern Argentina, with David as my assistant. I felt it right to say 'yes' as a way out of an impasse, subject of course to the agreement of Paraguay. David Leake and I were ordained bishops in Buenos Aires on St Thomas's Day, 21 December 1969, exactly 100 years after the consecration of the pioneer missionary Waite Hockin Stirling as the first Anglican bishop in the huge subcontinent of South America.

Immediately after the consecration service and a quiet Christmas I set off with Pat Harris for a three-week pastoral tour. Shendy and Andrew came with us. They relished getting up at five and driving up to the Chaco before the heat of the day. That trip included numerous confirmations. It wasn't long before I was crawling under the jeep, because something had gone wrong with the steering. When I muttered something about that being a good start in episcopacy, Pat responded in no uncertain terms, 'Don't think that we are going to let you change!' None the less, he took great care to present me to the people as their bishop. He noticed that in one village the folk had prepared a room with a bed for me to rest before the service. 'Part of your ministry', he said, 'is to let them make a fuss of you.' My pastoral tours usually took in three Sundays. Confirmations in the Chaco were planned by the day with no reference to the hour. Soon after my arrival they rang the bell, which was usually two or three feet of railway track hung from a tree or the building and the people would gather for a service.

The birth of SEAN

Tony Barratt, who moved with his family to Tucuman in Argentina, became increasingly focused upon the need for training church leaders. I had asked him if he would set up a seminary, but this had limitations. The existing church leaders were married men who needed further training but should not be taken away from their churches or their families for long periods. We needed to train on a broad base because the ministry in our churches was seldom concentrated on a single person. At that time few of our church leaders had much education beyond primary school where the tendency was to learn parrot fashion. How could we raise their conceptual ability? Instead of a correspondence course, we decided to use programmed textbooks with basic multi-choice questions, geared to a weekly seminar with a local leader, supported by a tutor's textbook. The range would be as comprehensive as most theological colleges. Tony cited the example of the Anglican Theological College at Kelham where the founder took students of varying abilities and made sure that they were introduced to the breadth of pastoralia and theology. We could do this through the preparation of well-illustrated step-by-step programmed manuals. Tony tested these out on each member of his family and if they could not remember 80 per cent of the material after two months, he judged that the fault lay in the book, not the student. Thanks to the support of the SPCK,[5] the first edition of the books was produced on an excellent duplicator in my garage. Tony suggested 350 copies; I argued for 1,000. While he was away we totalled both amounts, 1,350! A one-sided compromise if ever there was one! This was the comparatively small beginning for what we called SEAN, the Seminario por Extencion Anglicano. This became the Seminary by Extension to All Nations when SEAN took on its ecumenical and world-wide ministry. The pastoral compendium based on St Matthew's gospel so embraced the breadth of theology and pastoralia that over 70 missions and denominations now use it in numerous languages around the world. Many of us have thanked God that Tony Barratt was not diverted into the episcopacy, even if the Church could have done with at least one bishop who would not easily conform to its mould!

Towards national churches

There was significant growth and a move from missionary control to the indigenous church during 1971 and 1972. I wrote home about the visit of Canon and Mrs Harry Sutton for what was probably the last English-speaking conference of SAMS missionaries within South America: 'The missionary conference started here in Salta . . . with quite a packed programme. Sunday was a good day with the ordination of Terry Barratt in the morning and a most moving talk from Canon Leake in the afternoon, as he recounted some of his early experiences . . . I'm not sure if there will ever be another English-speaking staff conference like this one but I am sure that we must plan more and more for Spanish-speaking conventions. It is not good for missionaries to be discussing church policy.' I sometimes wondered how a small diocese, or even a church in England, would feel if it was blessed by an influx of foreign missionaries who none the less insisted on meeting in their own language to discuss and decide future plans for the local church.

A year later I wrote: 'The 120 churches we try to serve have approximately 5,500 communicant members and between them use seven different languages, Spanish being the most important, although the Guarani language in Paraguay and Mataco (Wichi) in northern Argentina, are widely used ... We were again impressed at the diocesan convention in Paraguay by the youth in our church. If we were problem-orientated our concern would be the obvious weakness of not having more mature leaders ... we are concerned to pray and do everything possible to help these young people prepare for increasing leadership in God's work in future.'

Then followed a note on Argentina: 'The diocesan convention in northern Argentina was timed around the national independence holidays (24–28 May). Two representatives from each of the 60 churches, plus other delegates, filled the marquee, queued for food, met in groups and slept! Highlights of the conference included the presentation (by the Argentine Bible Society's director) of the first copies of selected Old Testament portions in Mataco (Wichi) and parts of the New Testament in Toba. A tribute to the work of missionary and Indian translators, especially Canon Alfred Leake and the Revd Maurice Jones. As in Paraguay, youth was predominant among the representatives of the Spanish-speaking churches, but delegates from Mataco and Toba churches included men who had pastored their churches for many years. One encouraging aspect ... was the decentralization of the missionary! Someone commented, 'We have learnt that it doesn't matter if a missionary isn't around because we can consult together and take our problems directly to God.' Leaders in one area subsequently met and discussed how they can enable one of their pastors to have a full-time itinerant ministry.'[6] That led to the consecration of Mario Marino to be bishop in their area.

During all these developments I was called upon to represent our diocese, and to some extent the Anglican Church in Latin America, to the wider Anglican Communion. My first immersion (I was going to say dip of my toe!), into this came when David Reed, the dynamic North American bishop in Colombia and Monsignor Pironio, an outstanding Roman Catholic, called a meeting of ten Anglican and ten Roman Catholic bishops. I was asked to present an opening paper on the history of the Anglican Church up to and including the Reformation. We were shut up together in a monastery for ten days, although one night I did go out for a walk. The conference was like a Damascus road experience and I needed solitude to think! One elderly Jesuit bishop had poured his heart out about the confusion he felt. All his life he had been taught that we were heretics and now he was told to confer with us as brethren (albeit 'separated brethren'). In contrast another RC bishop quoted an Anglican theologian and seemed more evangelical in his doctrine of the eucharist than many Anglican bishops! A Roman Catholic adviser from Buenos Aires cited our work in the Chaco as an area where his church should recognize and encourage the Anglican work. We thought aloud in that conference and I learnt lessons and formed friendships which were invaluable in the coming years.

Marj and I were settled and contemplated taking on Argentine nationality, but Canon Sutton advised against this because he said we might be needed elsewhere. Indeed, in 1972 David Pytches, the bishop of Chile, Peru and Bolivia, approached us with a difficult request. He was concerned about the Anglican involvement in Peru and wondered if we could go there with a view to forming a new missionary diocese.

I visited Lambeth Palace to explain that there was excellent leadership potential for the different aspects of the work. Then after further consultation in the diocese it was agreed that Pat Harris would succeed me as bishop in northern Argentina and Doug Milmine agreed to go to Paraguay as the diocesan bishop there. We would be free to embark upon difficult and at the same time well worthwhile pioneering in Peru.

Notes

1 Australia has an even longer line of straight narrow gauge track.
2 Henry Grubb, *The Land between the Rivers*, USCL 1965, p. 13.
3 The previous bishop of Sao Paulo in Brazil also participated in the Anglican communion services.
4 Years later, a missionary bishop from central Africa told me that they were encouraged in following our policy in his own diocese.
5 SPCK is the Society for Promoting Christian Knowledge, the oldest Anglican missionary society, founded in 1698.
6 Letter home, 28 August 1972.

7
PERU

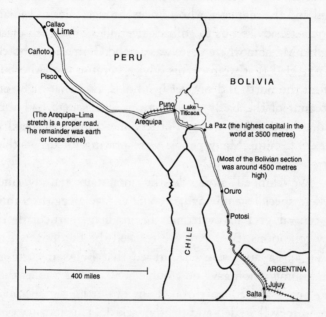

Callao
Lima
Cañoto
PERU
Pisco
BOLIVIA
(The Arequipa–Lima
stretch is a proper road.
The remainder was earth
or loose stone)
Puno
Lake
Titicaca
Arequipa
La Paz (the highest capital in the
world at 3500 metres)
(Most of the Bolivian section
was around 4500 metres
high)
Oruro
Potosi
CHILE
400 miles
ARGENTINA
Jujuy
Salta

The journey of a lifetime

Our departure from Salta at 4 p.m. on Friday 9 February
1973, was painful for all of us. We had grown to love
Argentina and it wasn't easy saying goodbye to our colleagues who had given us so much support and fellowship.
Joyce Illingworth kindly agreed to pack and post on my
books and we had reduced our other belongings to what
would fit inside the pick-up truck. The children took it in
turns to travel behind on top of the bedding box.

A thunderstorm broke just after we left and followed us all the way, off and on, to the next city, Jujuy, where the streets were like rivers. We were assured that it was local and pressed on to climb up the Andean foothills for an hour or so to a little town called Tilcara. The hotel was full and the manager, who I knew through sales of Indian artefacts, advised us to go back five miles to a small place called Mamara where there was a good German-run hotel. I was glad that we took his advice because even the bus from the north did not get in until 2 a.m. that night on account of the badly swollen river. The waters had sub-sided by the time we, and others ahead of us, reached it next morning. Many people were praying for us on that trip!

We climbed alongside the mountain railway line, where special steam engines could engage a cogwheel into a central grid to overcome the gradient, particularly in icy conditions. By 2 p.m. we reached the border town of La Quiaca and were encouraged that Bolivian customs and immigration gave no trouble at all. It was a relief that no one asked to go through any of our luggage because we were well loaded and tightly packed. 'This journey of a lifetime but only once in a lifetime!' so said Marj, as we were skirting around the worst of the sheer drops on the precarious bends of the mountain roads where all too frequent crosses marked the spots where vehicles had gone over the side. I resolved never to do it again. (But I did, by bus, 22 years later.) The weight of our load and prudent caution made progress slower than forecast and it took five hours of concentrated driving to cover the first 40 miles in Bolivia. We came across an isolated 'hotel' on one of the wider bends, at a place called Tojo. It was all a bit rustic and the provision of one candle, four beds and seven small chamber pots in our big room intrigued us. I think that we were too tired to ask for more candles and we did have our invaluable torches. Andrew, who was concerned lest his bike be stolen from the roof of the truck, slept in the cab.

We were on our way again by 7.30 a.m. and after another hour and 16 miles we reached the Bolivian Altiplano, at 5,000 metres. We would still face some mountain roads but most of our driving would be across the plains. One reason for choosing this route, rather than of going directly eastwards from Salta across the Andes into Chile, was that we would not have to carry petrol supplies on board. There was an ample supply of cheap petrol in Bolivia, usually from 40-gallon drums at isolated homesteads.

We were hoping to reach the historic mining town of Potosi that night, but just at sunset, after dropping down the zig-zag bends to a mountain valley, we found a car parked by a stream which had built up to a torrent. We had a tent and food. Several other cars arrived with no provisions and Marj found herself feeding 16 people on soup and long-lasting small hard buns called biscochos. We had brought a small primus, because unlike the Chaco there was not an abundance of wood for fires. The stream subsided and the other cars moved on around 5 a.m. It was well down after our breakfast at 7.40. By 10.30 we reached Potosi. I don't think I have ever felt so foreign as in that city. It seemed as if the ghosts of thousands of Quechuas who had died in the horrible history of forced labour in the mines were now haunting us through their descendants. People, especially children, just crowded round during the couple of hours we were getting punctures mended. I also bought a good jack. I soon needed it because Potosi's patches came unstuck and with Andrew's help I had to do them again.

Just before nightfall, after we had been negotiating deep ruts in the road all day, a lorry driver warned us to stay at the next small town, Chalapata, because a river further on was in flood and we would do well to cross it by day. People are so very helpful in these mountain areas. I found my turn came next morning when a couple of young French teachers could not get their little Citroen to go. We worked at it till nearly midday and then mended our own punctures. A Land Rover that had been towed through the flooded river the night before had been waiting several days for the water to go down. Even then it had come right up to the seats. But they said that the river was subsiding rapidly and it was a relief to us to find that the few extra hours had made all the difference. I knew that I could take off the fan belt to prevent water spraying over the electrics.

For safety and to lighten the loads, passengers from other vehicles were walking across the sleepers of a parallel railway bridge. Marj and the girls started to do the same, while Andrew accompanied me in the cab. Then he exclaimed, 'Dad, look at Mum'. We saw that she had 'frozen', through looking down between the sleepers at the rushing water below. Her childhood memories of seeing a drowned eight year old being pulled out of the sea had all flooded back. Andrew raced up to stand with them while I backed out of the river and fetched them back from the bridge. We returned to the car and all felt much more secure as we crossed together in the vehicle.

Worse was to come at the next wide river because the Chevy, which had only three forward gears of higher than average ratio, could not give the power needed for the shingle bed. We were stuck. A bus coming the other way pulled us back out, but understandably the driver did not want to turn around and spend time pulling us to the other side! As we sat on the river bank wondering what to do next, like unloading half our goods and coming back for the rest, I remembered that the Chevy had a more powerful reverse gear and we crossed the river backwards! The girls seemed to enjoy our unpredictable journey. Rossy said it was like a dream and was quite sure that it was a good dream! I did not share my secret nightmares of a flash flood catching us stuck in the middle of a river!

We liked the town of Oruro, where we were able to solve the puncture problem by purchasing two new tyres very cheaply! Later on we dropped 1,000 metres from the Altiplano down to La Paz, which claims to be the highest capital in the world. This was the only frustrating bit of the trip. We spent ages hotel hunting. My windscreen wipers were stolen and I had to buy second-hand replacements (which were probably my own!) in the market. I learnt the hard way that one should always remove windscreen wipers and protect vulnerable car lights against theft. This was especially true in Peru of Volkswagen Beetles. If metal guards were not fitted over the lights, these ended up looking like insects with their eyes gouged out! For many people a second-hand headlamp was worth more than a week's wage.

Our last hotel in Bolivia was just what we wanted. Like most of the others it was cheap, about £2.50 for the six of us, but it was also clean and the service attentive!

We set off early next morning to cross the border into Peru as soon as the customs opened, but we had not counted on the Bolivian customs official having a hangover from the night before. In the end, at about 9.30 a.m. the police official took me to his house to wake him up. I was afraid that I might have put him in a nasty mood but he noted down all our passport details and stamped us out. He forgot to check the car documents, though, and came panting across the bridge to catch us up while we were clearing our entrance with the Peruvian officials.

We continued around Titicaca (the highest navigable lake in the world) into Peru. People talked about the difficult roads ahead but I was glad that our stuff was safely through the customs into Peru; I could despatch a heavy drum and box by road. I was perturbed to discover that the road haulage companies sent their stuff on the top of long-distance buses. One missionary had seen a piano going that way!

It was midsummer and snowing as we dropped down the other side of the Andes and passed a sign indicating that at 4,600 metres we were alongside the world's highest railway. After going through Arequipa we began to smell the Pacific Ocean and that afternoon we headed north on a tarmac road up the coast to Lima. Sometimes we were at sea level, but I did not enjoy other parts where the road followed the sides of the cliffs with the ocean below. We promised ourselves that we would spend the last night of our journey in another good tourist hotel where we could enjoy hot baths and a rest before the final easy lap into Lima. We had not anticipated the weekend exodus of the more wealthy Lima residents to hotels in the coastal resorts. It looked as though we would end up in the tent

again when we found a basic hotel offering bed and breakfast in a large room with a cold water wash basin. So much
for languishing in a nice hot bath, or even a good shower.
I do not ever remember such exhaustion as Marj and I
dragged our feet around the town in search of bread and
a cooked chicken for our evening meal, having left the four
children asleep, all too tired to acknowledge their hunger.

Perhaps this is the right moment to confess that as the
years go on I feel ashamed of ever doing that journey, especially with the responsibility of the lives of the children.
I had not anticipated the dangers and at the time the
alternatives seemed much more complicated if we were to
arrive in Peru with our goods in time for the start of the
school year. Flying would have been the sensible answer,
even if it had increased the unhappy concerns about the
cost of initiating the work in Peru. The journey with its
mountains, rivers, hazards, matched by the tremendous
sense of God's direction, was a sort of microscopic picture
of the ups and downs with the blessings, which lay ahead
in Lima.

Problems and progress

Archbishop Michael Ramsey enthused over the map of
South America. I had spread it on the floor beside his big
armchair at Lambeth as I explained the proposal for our
move to Peru. Harry Sutton, who accompanied me on that
visit, enthused over the spirituality of the archbishop!

But not everyone was enthusiastic in Peru. In 1846 a
group had met in the British Legation and obtained permission from the Peruvian government for what would be
the first 'Protestant' services in that country. Permission

was granted, provided that no Peruvians attended and that the church building was hidden from the public. In 1848 Queen Victoria commanded her prime minister to appoint Pearson, the then incumbent of St Paul's, Newcastle upon Tyne, as the first Anglican chaplain in Lima. When he resigned as chaplain in 1874 the committee asked the Archbishop of Canterbury to appoint his successor. They wrote that Lima had 160,000 inhabitants. 'The religion of the country is Roman Catholic. No other is recognized or tolerated by law. Protestants are not molested in any way, but no church or building for the avowed purpose of Protestant worship has yet been erected in Lima.' The committee had started with the Queen and dropped down to the Archbishop of Canterbury!

Some of the church council who still seemed obsessed with status were hardly likely to jump for joy a century later when they were landed with me as bishop. A later chaplain, the Revd Arthur Robinson, who did much to establish good relationships, compared the feelings of the chaplaincy church in 1869 and 1973. 'The Anglicans of Lima were suspicious when "episcopal oversight" moved from London to the Falkland Islands and was exercised by Bishop Stirling with an evangelical missionary background. In fact, a striking parallel to this was to take place almost exactly one hundred years later, in 1973, when some residents expressed similar insecurity at the proximity of a bishop, whose background was missionary and evangelical, to a church which had long managed its own affairs far away from any other parish. In the 1970s, as in the 1870s, the bishop was only fully accepted as bishop when he had proved himself as a person.'[1]

The irony is that had they not made a fuss I might

have become much less involved in the chaplaincy church, but unlike Stirling, I was close enough to win and to woo. That was not difficult because misunderstandings aside we were surrounded by kind, supportive people, even if some of them could be awkward in committees! I cannot think of anyone in Peru who in the long term chose to be enemies and there was a nucleus of deeply spiritual people in the church. We were reaping the benefits of their prayers. Hard times lay ahead for the British community and it was our privilege to prepare for the future.

Missionaries and church leaders in other denominations cheered me with their generous advice and encouragement. I talked to the Cardinal, Archbishop Monsignor Landazuri Rickets[2] about the proposals, from the meeting of Anglican and Roman Catholic bishops in Colombia, that there should be much more mutual consultation and co-operation, and sought his counsel on where we might best commence work. True to his word he gave this some thought and replied through his ecumenical officer. While he would not want to recommend a specific area of work, he wanted me to know that if we opened any church he would like his representative to be present at the dedication ceremony. However, during my time in Peru we did not get around to constructing any proper church buildings, as most groups met in houses, or little rooms constructed of reed matting. Good roofing was not a priority when it only rained every seven years!

Stuart Harrison, the leader of EUSA (Evangelical Union of South America, now Latin Link) emphasized that the shanty towns around Lima represented the most unevangelized sections of Peru. An early EUSA missionary was the principal founder of the IEP (Iglesia Evangelica Peruana) which was planned to be the one evangelical denomination in the country. But painful splits ensued and I felt that there would have been more co-operation among the Baptist-orientated churches had they started, as in other republics, with the confident inheritance of their own history and doctrine. We were later able to help the IEP through a generous grant from the SPCK for the publication of an IEP hymnbook, which has since run into several reprints.[3]

A Methodist missionary asked us to respond to the request of a family who were asking for a church at a place called Pamplona Alta. This was one of the new settlements, or pueblos jovenes (youth towns). Over 50 per cent of the population was under the age of 15. Lima, which doubles its population every ten years, had its inner-city slums where people lived who had migrated from rural areas in search of work, education and health care. Then in the 1960s 40 families planned an overnight appropriation of land on the arid hillsides south of Lima. Middle-class people had already built on most of the agricultural land around Lima. In contrast these new settlers, in keeping with the Inca tradition, planned to settle on the desert hillside which was too high for irrigation. They quietly made the reed matting for their walls and roofs and hired lorries to take them out one night from the crowded inner-city slums to the higher land 20 miles south of Lima. By the next morning a settlement of 40 homes had appeared in a carefully ordered layout. Entrepreneurs provided water from the backs of lorries. Others joined them and relatives came in from the country, and the population of the pueblos jovenes, as they were called, now numbers several million people. Initially there was passive acquiescence from the authorities, but later on they gradually installed the basic services and service roads so that the shanty towns became acceptable suburbs.

In typical Anglican fashion I seemed to have a toe in all the camps! The ecclesiastical and political polarization surfaced acutely when a left-wing Methodist minister asked me if I would help him and the Lutherans in caring for refugees from Pinochet's repression in Chile. It was reported that the first to flee across the border at the northern Chilean town of Arica had been sent back and were among those who were summarily executed. The press ensured that Peru then opened its doors to future fugitives and the World Council of Churches channelled basic funding, pending more permanent settlements for many of them in Canada and Europe. Most of my friends in Lima were unhappy about my involvement, which could have been misconstrued as an endorsement of an extremely left-wing position. The Lutherans and I wanted to ensure that funds from Europe would be used with integrity for the support of destitute refugees, and a visit from the UN's Deputy High Commissioner for Refugees enabled us to get the relief operation on a trustworthy basis. He came to me for briefing before 8 a.m., reported back after 11 p.m. and had my Lutheran friend on the phone till well after midnight! That sort of commitment impressed me!

Thanks to the support of my colleagues, we had gradually formed a small missionary team. Bishop Pat Harris phoned me from Argentina saying that a new and very able missionary, Sheila Dale, would be willing to join us. Then Bishop Doug Milmine in Paraguay agreed to the transfer of Ada Barker and Sheila Haworth, plus a good Church Army couple, Ray and Beth Mills. Harry suggested that I approach the BCMS (now Crosslinks) about the possibility of their involvement in Peru and their first missionaries were Wilbur and Rosemary Kelly. He also asked me if we had a place for Paul and Esme Russel, who had previously worked in Chile. They soon built up a good congregation including young professionals with leadership potential in the middle class Vista Alegre[4] estate.

Some of our bishops argued that we should minister almost exclusively among the upper and middle classes but my conviction that we should also have a ministry among the underprivileged was reinforced by the arrival of the Mills, who moved out to the Pamplona area to establish a social work and several new churches.

The chaplaincy Church of the Good Shepherd was a good base for the start of our middle-class ministry. Some, including an army captain, were asking if there was a service in Spanish at the Good Shepherd and the church council agreed to us having Spanish-speaking services on Sunday evenings and on other occasions, providing that this did not clash with their timetable. The evening service in Spanish soon included a doctor, an accountant, several business people, an engineer and the son of a former prime minister.

Some members of the English community also came along, including Amy Griffis, who was a delightful lady and felt that her prayers were being answered in our ministry.

The Peruvian missiologist who encouraged me most was Dr Samuel Escobar. Until he entered the prestigious St Mark's University his faith had been fairly nominal, but so shamed was he by the commitment of the Communists that he emerged as an ardent and thoughtful Christian who challenged the conservative evangelicals to face up to the realistic evaluation of the root causes of poverty and oppression in Latin America.

Where next?

By the end of 1976 Marj and I had a growing conviction that we had taken our task as far as we could in Peru. I had become the first presiding bishop of the Anglican Council in South America (CASA), which incorporated our provincial structures including the appointment of bishops and formation of future dioceses. I felt my leaving would enable the province to own this with another presiding bishop. We were also concerned about our elderly mothers and two of our children back in England, who because they were not living with us at the time of our move, had not really identified with Peru. We pondered this and at one stage we both, unknown to each other, simultaneously wondered if we were running away from the difficulties. Then for a week I deliberately turned the thing on its head and thought hard of how things might work out if we stayed. I could get no peace on that score and when I shared all my pondering with Marj she said that she had been through the same process and had come out the other end with the same convictions.

So our minds were settled on what we believed to be the Lord's guidance. A lot of work lay ahead during the coming year, but there were the lurking questions of 'Where would we go?' and 'What would we do?' I received interesting suggestions of work from friends in the church office in New York and I was particularly attracted by a warm invitation from Archbishop Ted Scott in Canada, but neither of the possible posts met our responsibility to our family in England. Then Archbishop Donald Coggan suggested that I talk with Bishop David Sheppard of Liverpool, who, he said, needed some episcopal help. I met David at a Partners in Mission Conference in Kentucky and as I shared my thoughts he responded, 'You could be the answer to my prayers.' 'What', he asked, 'are your strong points?' I had never thought of strong points. I had perhaps worried too much about my weak ones! So my answer to David's question was: 'I can't think of many except that I have always been able to gather around me bigger and better people than myself for the task.' To which he replied, 'I'll settle for that.' And he did!

Our younger children have their own memories of Peru. Unknown to us, the girls 'liked to disturb a heap of cockroaches under the drain in the front patio from time to time'. 'Lima was so jolly mouldy' (due to the damp mist from the sea) and 'our shoes went green in the cupboard'. As did our clothes until we installed a low-watt heater in our wardrobe. Then there were 'the regular walks down to the rough beach' where Ros found 'a teeny baby seahorse', and the missionary days out when we got sunburnt and all ended up with 'white streaks of cream across our noses to prevent more damage'. The buses were 'always crammed full'. There were the 'black and white films we used to see at a cultural centre . . . George Formby films I remember . . .'

Our special bit of Peru

Over the years we had acquired a few bits of South American artefacts, but we said, 'This Christmas we must get something really Peruvian to take back with us to

England.' We little dreamt what, or rather who, that would be, when a couple from another mission phoned us to ask if they could come round for a confidential talk. I surmised that there must be some problems in their own mission because people occasionally felt that they could share such concerns with an Anglican bishop. We had no idea that they would ask us to help find a home for a little Peruvian baby boy just seven days old. The story was that his mother, who was more sinned against than sinner, could not keep him. We prayed with them and I said that we would keep praying and let them know if we could think of anyone. No sooner had they gone out of our front door when Marj and the three girls said, 'Why not us, why not us, Dad?'

For the first time in our family I was the one who was resisting an instant decision! I said that I would look into the legal position on adoption, which I did with Marj over the Friday and Saturday, by which time we had decided to say 'yes'. Marj told me that for some months she had had a conviction that God was going to give her a new responsibility and she soon realized that this was it. By nature I make decisions on what I believe to be right without giving enough thought to the problems that would have to be tackled. But on this occasion the responsibility was such that I felt I should put all the arguments on to paper. The arguments against were all of a selfish nature apart from my age. How would I relate to a teenager in my sixties? Arthur Robinson, the chaplain, and John Sutton both set me at ease. Arthur said, 'My father was old, but he was no less a father.' Our only regret was that we had been unable to consult with Shendy and Andrew back in England. It naturally took a little while to convince them that Mum and Dad were no madder than when they last saw them. Thirteen months later we were on our way to Liverpool with Tim, our special bit of Peru.

Notes

1 The Revd Arthur R. B. Robinson, *The Magnificent Field of Enterprise: Britons in Peru 1815–1915*, printed in Lima and published by the Author.

2 He told me that his mother was English and that he had been brought into the world in Arequipa by a missionary midwife of the Evangelical Union of South America (EUSA).

3 I was impressed by the fact that although it is often considered one of the more traditional Anglican societies, the SPCK responded so positively.

4 Meaning 'Gay View'. The word had not been hijacked by sexual innuendo at that time and is probably still OK in Spanish.

8
LIVERPOOL

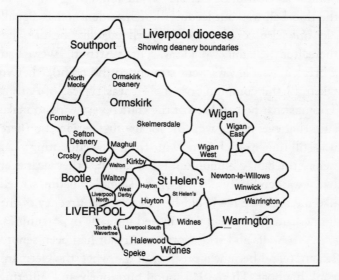

Down to earth

We arrived in our five-bedroomed Liverpool vicarage on Christmas Eve 1977. Shendy and Andrew had spent several days making a nice house into a lovely home, arranging the mixture of carpets, rugs and furniture that had been gathered together by friends in the dioceses. Bishop David Sheppard had supplied a vehicle and another surprise followed when the diocesan secretary mentioned that the parish had a £24,000 legacy invested in Church House.

The agreement was that after three months' settling in as vicar of St Cyprian's, Toxteth, I would give 50 per cent of my time to work as an assistant bishop in the diocese and the parish would have a senior curate, who became known as the associate vicar.

Arriving in Liverpool was a foretaste of heaven but I came down to earth with a bump at 7 a.m. on my first Sunday as vicar of St Cyprian's. The loud, long ringing of the doorbell was our leading churchwarden's crisis signal! No one else could make that bell talk like he did and thereafter the family would say, 'That's Arthur!' 'We've had a break-in' (he always went straight to the point), 'they've taken all the communion wine!' It was typical of Arthur Thomas that he had been at the church very early to make sure that everything was OK for my first service, so there was still time to fetch some wine from a neighbouring vicar before the 8.30 communion. I doubt if any other vicar ever had a warden like him. He looked like me, sometimes acted like me and like me could be ruled by the urgency of the immediate, but he had not enjoyed my early opportunities.

As a 'waifs and strays' orphan Arthur had been sent to sea at 16 and became a prisoner of war when the Germans sunk his boat. Then 1945 found him lonely and suffering from tuberculosis in a Liverpool sanatorium. Once cured he mitigated months of unemployment by hours of reading in a warm Liverpool library. Then he got a job in a piano factory and progressed to become the foreman.

Jack Roberts, our other warden, was completely different. A pleasant, easy-going, laid-back dreamer, he lived with his 90-year-old mother in the cluttered Dickensian drawing room of a big terraced house where once they had had two resident maids. It overlooked the old Botanic Park, which in Jack's childhood was a prestige area. By the 1970s most of the big houses had been converted into flats and the back streets were demolished.

Half the parish had post-war corporation houses, while

many of the remaining terraced houses had been tastefully modernized. Others had changed little over the years. Mr Pemberton, our previous university educated churchwarden, and his wife spent their evenings like Darby and Joan sitting in upright chairs, sometimes reading by gaslight, in front of an old-fashioned fireplace. I took our sprightly septuagenarian church secretary Josie home after a late parish church council meeting and discovered that, like that warden, she did not have electricity. 'Wait a minute, vicar,' she said, as she opened her door, 'I just have to light the light.' She then felt around in the dark for an upright chair, moved it to the centre of the room, climbed on to it, and struck a match to ignite the gas lamp.

David Alton, our MP and champion for the area, said that we had the highest proportion of outside toilets in Europe. He and I regretted that statement. A reporter came to me for an interview and I said that I would give it only if he reported the good things that were happening. He responded that he would write two articles, the down side first, to be followed up with the positive aspects of our parish. He portrayed the down side and quoted me as if that was all that I could see, but he never came back with the promised positive article! The attitude of the press towards Liverpool was similar to that of the prevalent attitude to the Third World. They could not see good people with problems, but only problem people, and it was then easy for them to preach blame and legislate from afar. Yet when I visited the Ford factory at Speke, the director, who had come from Dagenham, told me that he had the best work-force ever. 'The trouble is', he said, 'that every one of them is a comedian and the press will always get the story they want.' As I had learnt to my cost!

It was not intentional that I tripped up John Pugh,

the editor of the offending paper. We had become good friends when I responded to his challenge to race him to the car park up a back street of Manchester! As he said afterwards, 'It seemed a good idea at the time', but I accidentally caught his leg and he fell forwards as I tried to cut across behind him. I should have taken him to the hospital casualty department but his hunch that one of his junior editors would be lurking there looking for a good story worried him more than his wounds. Nor did I want anyone to report our capers! So his wife collected him from our home where Marj had bathed the bruises and the next day his dentist quietly fixed a broken tooth. I was too embarrassed to tell the story until now.

Canon Lindsay, a legendary vicar, had built up our parish in the 1940s and increased the church seating to 930. But inner-city church life had sunk to a low ebb by 1979. Sixty per cent of the population had left the area. Some, like our Boys' Brigade leader, had been bombed out during the wartime blitz and many of the slightly better off later moved out to the suburbs. Several thousand were decamped from substandard houses as the bulldozers moved in. The Christians among them reinforced the growth of suburban congregations, while hardly any new members joined our congregation apart from a few brought in by the Boys' Brigade. Their company, the 43rd, had once been the largest in England.

Community at St Cyprian's

I was attracted to St Cyprian's because it seemed to be on its uppers and things would turn around, thanks to the faithfulness of the congregation and the ministry of my colleagues Phil Miller and Ricky Panter. And a little inspired opportunism helped! At the end of my first Sunday Arthur said, 'I've got four baptisms for you next Sunday afternoon.'

'Arthur', I replied, 'I have some difficulty with that. I don't want to start changing things, but I would much prefer to have the baptisms during the morning service.'

'But I've already fixed it and they are coming!'

'Never mind, give me their names and addresses and I will visit each one to chat about the baptism and see if they mind the change.'

That Monday I learnt that we still had a strong community. All the mums whose babies I would baptize had gone to school together. It was a matriarchal society – look out if you got on the wrong side of granny. Thankfully the first mum was happy with the proposals and understood that I wanted them to feel that they belonged to the congregation. Her word reached the others before I knocked on their doors. The unforeseen bonus was that the extended families, which came for the baptisms, doubled the size of our congregation on my second Sunday in the parish. Nothing succeeds like success and word went round that our congregations were growing! So we set the first Sunday of the month as a family service with baptisms and encouraged newcomers to attend then. There was plenty of room, with over 800 empty seats! It was this that made me think of the sacraments of holy communion and baptism as God's instruments of mission and affirmation, whereas the Church has often made them tools for discipline. People interpret that as rejection and our community had already suffered enough of that elsewhere without the Church joining in. When it fell to my lot to sort out misunderstandings over baptism I tried to show that we wanted the very best for their babies: 'If you want me to, I will baptize your baby, so let's not argue over that, but first of all can I tell you what it is all about.' Only then did the message get through.

People told me that Canon Nixon, the last vicar but two, had visited every home in the parish during his first 18 months and I suggested that we should form a visiting team to repeat the exercise. 'But Vicar', they said, 'we are not trained like you.' Not being a parson could be an advantage and I begged them not to try to imitate the quasi-theological patter of Jehovah's Witnesses. 'Be natural, just tell them that you are from St Cyp's and want to know if we can be of any help to them.' Around ten volunteers met to pray each Sunday afternoon before we set out on our visits. To ensure effective coverage we prepared forms with the street name and house number and, where we knew it, the occupant's name. Key questions included, Did they happen to belong to any church? Did they have older folk who were lonely? Were there youngsters who might be interested in the Boys' Brigade or Sunday school? Would they like a visit from the vicar? As a simple commitment to follow up we asked if they would like to get the church magazine. I saw this as pre-evangelism and people would not start attending church immediately. But some did, including a future churchwarden. That programme with its follow up kept us busy for a couple of years.

The distribution of our monthly magazine soon increased from 100 to 450, and then 600. We charged a nominal price, which gave a reason to knock on the door and ask how things were. Our two lay readers, Sam Smart (an ex-long-distance lorry driver who described himself as

the first 'cloth cap reader in the diocese') and Harold
Morris (a more traditional former teacher), were a great
help in pastoral visits to all our church members. Apart
from three days taking chocolates to clergy widows I was
almost free of diocesan duties in the three weeks before
Christmas, so I was able to call on everyone who received
the magazine. We also put a Christmas card through every
letterbox. Guest services to bring people in could be a bit
threatening unless the invitation came at a natural time
like Christmas, Easter or Harvest Festival and we knew
that our card at Christmas would be welcome.

Our large Victorian church building on the corner of
Edge Lane and Holt Road was, and still is, an anchor site in
a parish which has had more than its share of dereliction
and demolition. When the scaffolding went up in preparation for cleaning, one man stopped his lorry and came
into the church. 'You're not going to pull it down? They
have closed so many others already.' I assured him that
thanks to a legacy, a community service scheme and a co-
operative architect who was prepared to work with volunteers
at a reduced fee, we were able to renovate the interior.
Church members installed a new heating system, put in
sound amplification and rewired the church. We still had
seating for 400 after providing a kitchen, three meeting
rooms and an upstairs hall.

The congregation was hard-working and generous. Most
survived on unemployment payment or basic pensions yet
on any Sunday the rattle of coins in the collection plate
was subdued by the prevalence of notes. Before we had a
second outbreak of dry rot in the roof, we were hoping to
raise our giving to mission from its basic 10 per cent to
nearer 50 per cent of our income.

My colleague Ricky Panter was leaving in the summer of 1985 and he put it to me that the parish was at the stage where it would be better if the vicar was full time. So after consultation with the diocesan staff we moved 15 miles across the city to Christ Church, Waterloo where the set-up made it easier for me to serve the diocese. Since then St Cyprian's parish has experienced increasingly difficult years. The double murder of Sharon Lester and her baby daughter not far from the vicarage hit the media in 1998. That tragedy brought the total of violent deaths in the parish to seven within a twelve-month period. But the social and spiritual ministry of the church has grown and my successor, David Lewis, is gallantly responding to the need for further improvements in the building.

Diocesan dimensions

Thanks to Bishop David Sheppard's careful planning and support I was pressed but not crushed with the work. He ensured that we were masters of our diaries, which we co-ordinated in two six-hour sessions each year. In May we pencilled in our major commitments for the coming year, starting with about 103 days for holidays and time off! That seemed a lot until I totted up the total of the normal weekends, bank holidays and annual holidays in the secular world. Space for deskwork, reading weeks, 'catch-up' days and quiet days was the next priority. These items could be moved but not removed. The timing of major diocesan and ecumenical events, like six meetings a year with other church leaders, would be checked with diocesan officers and ecumenical partners. Then in July we would sort out the confirmations and specific requests from parishes and further afield.

The 'catch-up days' provided flexibility for crisis situations. David would do his utmost to visit the vicarage immediately in the case of family disasters or serious sickness, even if that meant some of his precious diary time had to go out of the window. Clergy had his ex-directory telephone number and if they were in difficulty he would see them if need be after 10 p.m.[1] at the end of a busy day.

Liverpool has experienced contrasting episcopal styles. Bishop Martin watched everything and the diocesan secretary logged all phone calls, which he would then scan on a weekly basis. In contrast, his much-loved successor Stuart Blanch had a hands-off approach. He listened carefully to the concerns of one of his staff before he put his arm around his shoulder and said '. . . you've got problems', which provoked the reply, 'Bishop, you don't delegate, you abdicate.' David Sheppard did not abdicate but he was a master at delegation. We valued his advice, but he let us get on with the job. This would usually be reviewed at our annual joint work consultation. His choice of Michael Henshal as the bishop of Warrington could not have been better for the diocese. I appreciated Michael's advice on parish administration during my early days, when a brief telephone call would elicit more insight than a chapter in a book on pastoralia. His commitment to mission and ministry plus flexibility in parish churchmanship meant that even the most evangelical of parishes involved him in parish life. Most of us assumed he would be made a diocesan bishop elsewhere. When that did not happen David's comment was, 'All I can say, Bill, is that God is being very good to Liverpool.'

Our diocesan staff meeting was a highlight in my diary. The area deans took it in turns to brief us about the ministry and concerns of the clergy, including those who might be overlooked because they quietly got on with the job without drama or disaster. In spite of getting an average of 80 letters a day David was able to recall things clergy had written years before. He was also very good at forgetting past misdemeanours, particularly if a clergyman had come clean at the time. He did the ordinary things extraordinarily well and had little time for what he would call a lazy letter.

The bicycle or the lost boat

Between us we took over 120 confirmation services a year. One reason why there were so many candidates was that confirmations produced more confirmations. Friends and relatives present would be in a receptive mood and some would come forward next time round. Numbers varied from 67 in a single Wigan parish to just two or three in an inner-city group. Two parishes that should have combined did not have space for everyone who wanted to attend. My diary was so full that at their suggestion I took two services, in two crowded churches, on the same evening, one at 6.30 p.m. and the other at 8 p.m. It was not ideal, because I missed mixing with the first congregation and encouraging the newly confirmed afterwards.

As work increased I was greatly blessed with the help of voluntary drivers, particularly Albert Sutton who, prior to his retirement, had covered 40,000 miles a year. It was such a relief to walk out of the office and give quiet thought to the coming service while he got me there. Albert didn't seem to mind the same confirmation sermons, but one night he asked, 'Is it the bicycle or the lost boat tonight?' The bicycle had to do with the reasonableness of faith in putting God to the test when we see it working in others. The other story was of a boy who, looking in a second-hand shop, spotted his beautifully home-made sailing boat with its miniature sails, which had carried it away on a calm sea. He saved his pocket money to buy it back and as he walked home with the precious possession on his arm he was heard to say, 'You are twice mine, twice mine, I made you and I bought you.' Mine by creation and mine by redemption. That fitted my favourite confirmation text: 'Christ Jesus has made me his own.'

A healing ministry

The press had pounced upon the unguarded remarks of one of the two diocesan exorcists who had been appointed by Bishop Stuart Blanch, and David Sheppard was under pressure to inhibit the ministry of exorcism. We talked about this at one of our three 'bishops' days' and David asked me if, on his behalf, I could take a positive lead in a ministry of healing, which would embrace services for deliverance from evil. We delayed going public for six months so that I could read books, attend study conferences and consult leading churchmen, including Roy Lawrence, whose healing services had received positive affirmation in some Granada television programmes. I also got to know the sources of strength within the diocese so that the bishop could appoint an advisory panel of psychiatrists, general practitioners and clergy of different theological out-look.

What amazed me in St Cyprian's was that some folk

who on the surface had no problems were the first to kneel for prayer. Some like Amy experienced physical healing. Within a few days of coming forward she greeted me on the street with the words, 'Vicar, me ulcers be gone, me ulcers be gone!' Others, like our warden Stan, who experienced no physical change, told me later of the tremendous comfort and strength they drew from the laying on of hands and prayers. Indeed, to quote Roy Lawrence, 'Those who were not healed, often seemed to experience most blessing through the service.' We encouraged local clergy to take a lead themselves with a quiet confidence in the power of God's Holy Spirit. Sometimes a nervous vicar would press for my presence when parishioners found a part of their house haunted by a dark and frightening feeling. This feeling was often confined to a room where bad experiences, even a murder, may have taken place. We avoided sensationalism and publicity but nothing convinced me of the power of God's goodness over evil like being pushed into this ministry.

The cathedral of Waterloo

The ethos of Christ Church, Waterloo, our new parish, was completely different from the casual atmosphere of St Cyprian's, Toxteth, where some people would say, 'Hi ya bish', as they passed me on the pavement. In contrast, older folk in Waterloo were more likely to doff their caps, even if I was on my bike! But the former glory was fading. Many of the huge houses had been converted into flats or nursing homes, as the wealth moved away. Vernon, a retired headmaster who had taught almost all of our members, could remember the horse-drawn conveyances of wealthier worshippers at the now redundant massive church building (nicknamed the cathedral of Waterloo). The parish had been so well endowed that all the collections were given to missionary and other charitable societies.

What we inherited was an invaluable band of willing, able people, like Vernon, who were looking with imagination to the future, while keeping a foot in the past! The two wardens, Ronny Kynaston and Derek McLoughlin, who had worked together each week on the maintenance of the old church, now took equal care of the church hall which had been converted into a beautiful worship centre. The churchwardens knew that Deaconess Dorothy Hankey would be my full-time assistant and willingly agreed that I would give increasing time to the diocese.

Dorothy virtually ran the parish. She worked hard at visiting, including elderly Christians in the various nursing homes. She took the bread and wine from our Sunday communion to many folk for little services that indicated to the housebound that this was a sharing with the congregation, which they could no longer join in person. It wasn't long before some were asking why she could not take the whole communion service. I had no doubt that when the time came for the ordination of women she would be welcomed and accepted even by the more conservative church members.

It seemed that at last we would go through to retirement without another move. Friends asked my advice about who might be the next general secretary of SAMS and I was quite clear in my mind that this was not for me. Apart from all the satisfaction of my situation I felt that it would be wrong to put Marj on the spot about what might be a costly decision. The parish was building an attractive new vicarage for us and plans were formulating for the future. There were also financial implications because the diocese paid me as an assistant bishop and we were saving towards housing in retirement. But Marj was listening to the Lord. Out of the blue she said that she was sure that SAMS would ask me to do the job and if they did, I should take it. When I mentioned what it would do to our budget she asked, 'Since when did we make money a factor in doing the Lord's work?'

Later that week I had given a positive reference for a local vicar who was applying for the job when, as Marj had predicted, a letter came from Michael Cole, the SAMS chairman, asking me if I would apply for the post. David Sheppard helpfully made me think hard about all the adjustments that I would have to make. I was not sure how SAMS would respond to my convictions on world mission today and the adjustments needed within the society, but after an initial meeting with a small group from SAMS we warmed to the challenge and I knew that I should not run away from the job.

When the difficult moment came for me to talk with the churchwardens at Christ Church just nine months after my induction as their vicar, they could not have been kinder or more understanding. Derek set me at ease by saying, 'Before you came we were afraid that we would be shut down, but now we know that we are all right!'

Note

1 That also became known as the best hour for clergy to get us on the phone, even if, in my case, I was sometimes sitting up in bed playing Scrabble with Marj.

9

TUNBRIDGE WELLS

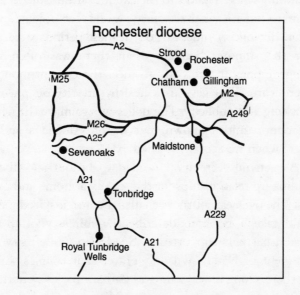

Rochester diocese

Partnership in practice

SAMS always seemed to be under financial pressure; yet in the goodness of God I do not remember any occasion when the society turned down a new opportunity because it did not have the money. The vision at home was matched by a willingness on the part of the missionaries to live very modestly. At one stage when Harry Sutton indicated that the society might have to reduce the number of missionaries it was planning to send, those who were working in Argentina made it clear that they would prefer a reduction in stipend to a cut-back in the programme.

The pre-1949 decline of SAMS with the post-war devaluation had left the society almost bankrupt. Then the subsequent growth from 30 to over 120 missionaries, with expansion into new areas, meant that all new money was absorbed in expanding work. Thanks to the careful stewardship of Phil Tadman, our financial secretary, we did not become overdrawn during my time, but our leanest periods were just after the summer holidays when there was often just enough money in the bank to meet the current month's expenditure. That gave us a healthy priority on praying, preaching and publicity. The policy was to make the needs and opportunities known, but we only made a special appeal when we actually needed extra money.

As general secretary I needed to be out and about, building up relationships for the society at home and overseas. The overseas journeys challenged and inspired me. It would take a book to describe the ministry of all the mission partners supported by SAMS. In Chile I saw the fulfilment of Daddy Wilson's prayer that couples would stay there a long time. Colin and Barbara Bazley went there in 1962. He became a bishop in 1969, and under his leadership evangelism has reached out across social classes and the Anglican Church has a ministry in every major city. In Paraguay I saw how some of the groups we had started had church buildings, and Bishop Doug Milmine, who was succeeded by John Eddiston, had negotiated the funding for Indian settlements on tracts of land alongside the Chaco road. In Peru I greatly admired the courage and tenacity of Bishop Alan Winstanley and his team as they pressed quietly on in spite of the violence and the threat of a bloodbath, had the Shining Path guerrilla movement gained the upper hand.

It was good that when some missionaries had to leave northern Argentina at the time of the Falkland/Malvina war there was a surge in national leadership under Bishop David Leake. It was also timely that Kath Clark, our assistant general secretary, and I had both served in South America and were fluent in Spanish because in addition to time spent with the missionaries we were much more involved with national leaders in all the republics. I enjoyed staying with them and listening to their concerns.

Umberto Axt, now the suffragan bishop in northern Argentina, pulled no punches. 'When you were here you emphasized that SAMS must listen and respond more to the national leaders. How do you feel now that you are the general secretary of SAMS?' I assured him that my convictions had not changed, even if I was no longer a presiding bishop in South America but a representative of a missionary society. Whereas my 1951 contract described me as an agent of the South American Missionary Society, we now described SAMS as an agent of the churches in South America and the Iberian Peninsula. To clarify this the general council accepted four principles of operation, which my successor Bishop David Evans has described as SAMS's vision for the future: 'To be an agent of multi-way International Mission . . . to shift the focus away from sending mission partners to supporting national mission . . . to represent the Church of South America to the Church in the UK', and 'to take appropriate initiatives in partnership with other mission agencies'.

These principles helped relationships with the church leaders in Brazil. SAMS was insisting on missionary teams for mutual support, whereas the Brazilian bishops felt that missionaries should be spread around and become more integrated with the local church. I worked with Canon Jubal Neves, the provincial secretary of the Brazilian Episcopal Church, on advisory groups for the Anglican Consultative Council. After our first meeting, in Australia, he urged the bishops to keep the doors open for SAMS missionaries. Over the years their evangelical ministry has been effective and appreciated by the Brazilian church while, as a missionary society, we had much to learn from Brazil in preparation for the adjustments as nationals replace missionary bishops in the SAMS areas of the Southern Cone.

I met Ian and Simea Meldrum in north-east Brazil, at Recife. They introduced me to different aspects of their ministry among the poor. Simea had graduated as an architect prior to study in preparation for her ordination and has used both skills to good effect in the church. They showed me the ancient cathedral of one of my heroes, Archbishop Helder Camara. He had summed up the pressure he felt by saying, 'When I feed the poor they say I am a saint, but when I ask why the poor are hungry they call me a Communist.' On the eve of my departure for England, Simea's parents treated us to a very late meal in a fish restaurant on a pier looking over the Atlantic towards home.

Philip King, my predecessor, had built up good relationships with the Reformed Episcopal Church in Spain and the Iglesia Lusitania in Portugal, both of which have become full members of the Anglican Communion. Our involvement in the Iberian Peninsula presented other exciting opportunities, particularly when Bishop Arturo Sanchez saw the potential of Rogelio Prieto's contribution to theological education in Spain. Then, in partnership with Crosslinks and the diocese of Chile, we helped to finance Juan Zamorra and his wife as Chilean missionaries to Spain. That sort of co-operation in multi-way mission avoided the danger of a national worker feeling owned and beholden to a single mission agency.

Policies in practice

We had a super SAMS UK team, which was usually patient with me, but if I had my time again I would refrain from initiating decisions during my first three months. These could have been better spent talking with each member of the staff about their work and aspirations.

I had not changed much since the days when someone described me as a young man in a hurry. But it is not easy to hurry a large organization, and over the years the governing structure of SAMS had grown from a small general committee to a 30-strong council with various committees, sub-committees and working parties, most of which created activity rather than action. A lot of frustration was avoided when we were able to clarify that the purpose of the general council had to do with the policy of the society. A small group of trustees (between ten and 12) would hold legal responsibility and form a bridge between the council and the executive staff, whose job it was to put policy into practice. I had hoped to maintain a permanent presence of a Latin American leader on the SAMS UK staff, because our decision-making had a good overseas perspective during the year that Miss Susie Tapia joined us from Peru.

We rejoice in the way in which my successor David Evans has been able to build on the policies and procedure which we were able to establish during our six years in the SAMS

HQ, and thank God for the privilege of being able to serve there. We owe so much to SAMS, who were flexible enough to accept me as a 22 year old and give me and Marj so much trust and support over the years, so I suppose it is understandable that SAMS is still very dear to our hearts.

My final South American visit on behalf of the society was to Brazil, when Jubal Neves invited me to be one of the sponsors at his consecration as bishop. It was a poignant occasion because my dear friend Archbishop Olavo Ventura Luis had contracted and died from a form of cerebral malaria, following a visit to Angola and South Africa. As Jubal knelt for his ordination, it was Bishop Olavo's widow who placed her late husband's pastoral staff into his hands. Then the children gave Jubal their father's other symbols of office as a bishop.

10
NEWARK

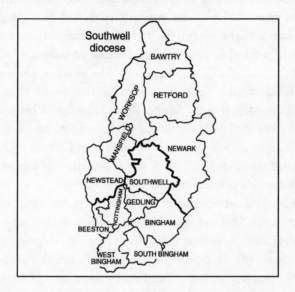

Southwell diocese

BAWTRY

WORKSOP

RETFORD

MANSFIELD

NEWARK

NEWSTEAD

SOUTHWELL

NOTTINGHAM

GEDLING

BEESTON

BINGHAM

WEST BINGHAM

SOUTH BINGHAM

Serving in the Southwell diocese

Bishop Pat Harris kindly invited us to plan for retirement in the diocese of Southwell, with the option of a few years in full-time work. We found a retirement home in Newark and the diocese had asked if someone could support their three full-time funding advisers by teaching the principles of stewardship. My first reaction was that I did not want to be a begging bishop, but there was no need to beg because the funding advisers were doing such excellent work in helping parishes to draw up budgets and meet their commitments. My job would be to preach the liberating gospel of generosity because until people enjoy giving generously they do not possess, but are possessed by their possessions.

Pat also asked me if I would serve the diocese as an adviser in rural ministry. This was better than a dream come true. As a young missionary I had thought that perhaps I might spend the tail end of my ministry as a vicar in a rural English parish. I knew, of course, that my father's hope that I might become the vicar of my native Mudford would never do, even if the parish became vacant, which it didn't! The Revd Douglas White, who went there in 1949, continued till he was 90 and became the longest serving incumbent in England. He found it a strain at the end. Rural parishes are no longer places where tired parsons can be put out to grass.

Canon Valerie Rampton is typical of recently appointed rural vicars. She has three parishes which, including extra hamlets, have four church buildings and five congregations. She also holds the post of Diocesan Adviser in the Ministry of Women. Valerie introduced me to some lovely Christian farmers and their families. Like most bishops I loved visiting housebound folk who have lifelong links with the local church. Valerie took me to a 90-year-old blacksmith's widow and we talked about the 'good old days' before I prayed with her. When her daughter met Valerie the following week she said, 'Mother is going senile. She swears black and blue that a bishop came to visit her last Tuesday!'

I also enjoyed serving as an adviser in world mission. I preached a bit and pontificated a bit more. The representatives of the Anglican Mission Agencies met regularly to plan events like deanery missionary weekends. Visitors from overseas would come for a combined event on the

Saturday evening, and then preach in various churches on
the Sunday.

One last fling

During one holiday Tim and I travelled back to the land
of his birth. We chose the cheapest way of seeing as much
of South America as possible within a month. We flew to
Sao Paulo in Brazil and spent 13 days, plus nine nights,
crossing the continent on buses and trains via Paraguay,
northern Argentina and Bolivia into Peru, where we would
eventually meet his birth mother before flying home from
Lima.

It was a journey full of emotions. Tim saw real poverty
for the first time as we visited one of the favelas in Sao
Paulo.[1] We were captivated by the extensive and impressive
Iguazu Falls, as we walked half a mile along the side of a
ravine and saw the huge and small jets of water crashing
down between seemingly small trees and islands on the
opposite side. The forest atmosphere has not been obliterated
by provision for tourists and quite large snakes are likely to
cross the footpath and slither off into the humid vegetation.

Satellite discs seemed to have sprung up like lonely
upturned mushrooms across Brazil. That evening we
watched an international football match on multi-television
screens in the bus terminal as we waited for our midnight
'executive' bus for Asuncion. There I met some old friends
and rested before crossing to Argentina and the Chaco. I
felt relaxed as for the first time I was a sort of tourist in
South America with no responsibilities in my old diocese,
but Tim said, 'Nobody seems to have told them that, Dad.'
It was a privilege to preach, visit and pray for sick folk. We

stayed in our old home with David and Shelly Stokes who are responsible for the ongoing training of Indian church leaders. Alec Deane, an Argentine agricultural missionary, has encouraged the Indians to carve beautiful birds and animals from the hardwood of the scrub forest. Wooden benches with a small vice, plus a saw, wood file, sandpaper and methylated spirit for polishing the finished article have appeared in the shade outside of almost every home in the community. Alec now spends his time finding enough markets to keep those craftsmen on the go and I promised to do what I could in retirement. That has become a major project, with sales exceeding £46,000 to date.

I am not the only ex-missionary to be involved in the ongoing support of the mission. Some like Phil Craft and Dr Michael Patterson with his wife Virginia have gone back for a treasured ministry in retirement. Bob Munday gave up his UK dental practice to work for a pittance (by English standards) in the Chaco. He drove us down to the provincial capital of Salta where we spent a couple of days in our old home there before retracing the 'journey of a lifetime' described in Chapter 6. We were taken in buses almost non-stop for 60 hours to La Paz in Bolivia. Three more days' travel got us to the ancient Inca capital of Cuzco and then Machupicho, the lost city of the Incas, followed after more sightseeing by a bumpy cold night journey to Arequipa before we went up the coast to Lima.

Never have I seen such a transformation in the ethos of a city as that following the capture of Anibal Guzman, the Shining Path rebel guerrilla leader in Lima. The police and army had scoured the country only to find him a few blocks from the central police station. On my previous visit I had seen shops functioning in the suburbs with iron grilles across the doorway to avoid armed hold-ups. The goods were sold through the grille to customers standing on the pavement outside. Such was the state of siege atmosphere. All this had been transformed in two or three years with supermarkets opening up and a sense of progress on all sides.

We had allowed a full week in Lima before our flight, just in case of delays on the journey. We stayed with Basil Whitehorn and his wife who were serving the English chaplaincy during their retirement. It was lovely to visit congregations and meet so many friends.

We were puzzled by the height of the effigies of ancient Inca rulers in the museums in Lima. We thought that all the Amerindians had been short to middling. Then the next day Tim met Carmen, his birth mother. Her first words after the embrace were, 'You are tall just like your father.' She explained that he was from the Inca line, and the Incas were tall. Tim was of course thrilled to know that he had the blood of the ruling class and remembered the insistence of his first schoolteacher that he was a descendant of a ruler.

Carmen's three other children joined us for a special meal, which she had prepared in the home of her former employers Paul and Marti Clark of the Scripture Union. Then we went to the pueblo joven where Carmen and her family lived. Uncles and aunts also gathered and because they are an extended Christian family it wasn't long before they were singing hymns and praying. The time came for us to leave. Tim was happy to find his original roots and Carmen was thrilled to see the son she had given up for adoption 18 years before. They have met since, when she joined in a study expedition as a Quechua translator. Tim had organized this as an undergraduate at Magdalene College, Oxford. It was not so easy without the other siblings present, as she wanted to mother him as a long-lost son. But one cannot turn the clock back 20 years and that trip, and time alone in the highlands of Peru, helped Tim to sort out who he is and what he would do with his cultural roots firmly established in this country.

Retirement

I thought that I was beginning to feel the strain at 67 and decided to retire. I had allowed myself to attend too many committees and write reports, neither of which is my forte. The only difficulty at this stage is not having enough time to do everything and the feeling that it does take longer to get things done. I have more hope of finishing off some improvements in our retirement home. The sale of the native craftwork from Argentina continues to grow and rather reluctantly I am being pushed towards the formation of a charitable company as it expands beyond the scale of our philanthropic association. But the fact that every two or three items sold means an extra day's work for one of my Wichi friends makes it all worthwhile, plus the ability to return all the profits for use in the area where the items are made.

When Archbishop George Carey graciously awarded me with the Cross of St Augustine I was reminded that nothing I have done could have been achieved but for the grace of God, and with the marvellous support of so many colleagues. If I had my time again I would not want different parents, a different wife, or a different family. Nor would I have wanted a different life. The good Lord has protected us from potential disasters and given us precious friends and colleagues along the way.

Preparing this book brought computers into my life and the Internet enables me to link up with Christians around the world. The morning hour of prayer and Bible reading plus our family prayers, when Marj and I always used *Daily Light*, became very precious. As I now face whatever the future holds I recall a little prayer along these lines:

If I no more my comfort draw from my firm
   grasp on Thee
Then may I know throughout it all, Thy mighty
   hold of me.

At the end of the day it is not so much great faith in God as faith in a great God which matters.

Note

1 Favelas are very poor suburbs which start as squatter settlements, usually on the hillsides surrounding the Brazilian cities.